HISTORY AS A HUMAN SCIENCE

The Conception of History
in Some Classic
American Philosophers

Victorino Tejera

UNIVERSITY
PRESS OF
AMERICA

LANHAM • NEW YORK • LONDON

All University Press of America books are produced on acid-free
paper which exceeds the minimum standards set by the National
Historical Publications and Records Commission.

To Justus Buchler

"Lack of historical sense is the original error of all
philosophers."

Nietzsche (HATH 1878)

HISTORY AS A HUMAN SCIENCE

The Conception of History in Some Classic American Philosophers

Chapter I

Introduction by Way of James and Dewey

The Societal Nature of the Human Agent

Philosophic historiography is, to put it minimally, a partly historical activity. The account that follows will, therefore, be both historical and as fully reflective as possible. Not to be historical about matters to which there is a historical dimension is to be less than fully reflective. It is also to beg the question of the nature of philosophy of history, as self-styled philosophers of history do who start out by assuming that theirs is a purely epistemological inquiry rather than inquiry or query of some other, or mixed, kind (FHK 1965, APH 1965, OKHP 1973).

This difficulty, however, is avoided by those who include sociology of knowledge in what they mean by epistemology, and who recognize in practice that sociology involves historical query. Some recognize, in fact, that the production of sociological knowledge, like the production of other knowledges, is a historical process. Philosophic historiography, in other words, is required to monitor its own procedures; it is required to be self-reflective as well as reflective about its subject-matter.

Insofar as every science is pursued or practiced by humans, any science is a "human science." Knowledge of anything, in any order, is knowledge of that thing in human terms--no matter how reductive our special-science terminologies may be, or how well they succeed in neutralizing personal conditions in the research situation. So, if the aim of intellectual history is to clarify the ongoing process of practical and productive human activity, this history will be a "human science" or "techne" in some additional senses. It will be an account (in human terms) of what we call distinctively human activities and achievements.

But since these cannot be documented without an implicit judgment as to how well they were carried through, history will also be an implicitly evaluative enterprise. This means that history, including the history of the natural and theoretical sciences, cannot be an entirely theoretical endeavor. To be the latter, it would have to be history _not_ addressed to practice or production. To the degree that histories of natural science have been concerned with the conditions under which the natural sciences have changed, to that degree have have they attended to the practical and productive contexts of theory. Of course, to the extent that reflective practice adds to our store of understanding, and we treasure understanding for its own sake, to that extent history is theoretical.

[The reader may want to be reminded that the "technes" in Aristotle's usage are for the sake of practice or production. They are what we would call arts-and-sciences. "Theories" in Aristotle are for the sake of understanding alone (EN, PA). "Science" is a Latinate term and not Aristotelian: for Aristotle, science in the sense of warranted knowledge is not restricted to theory but includes the practical know-ledges as well as reflective production.]

When the project is to study the distinctively human activities, what are the assumptions which it appears necessary to make or revise? We ask because it has become clear that our understanding of these acti-vities has been distorted by the distinctions with which they have been separated out and categorized. Hasn't human responsiveness been misconceptualized, if it is assumed that there is some point in the human constitution at which the physical and the animal break off and spirituality and humanity begin? Is not the response of an individual always of the individual as a whole, no matter how fragmented he or she might be and no matter how insufficient the response might be to the total situation or to the potentials of the individual?

A human being not only "experiences" his life, there is an extent to which he "makes" it. He proces-ses, assimilatively and manipulatively, whatever he encounters. He does this with his malleable, informable (conditioned and reconditionable) natural endowment and with the equipment he has internalized from his cul-ture. When the human process is viewed in this way, the old "stimulus-response" analysis of behavior becomes inadequate and the notion of "experience" associated with it reveals its insufficiency as a basis for accur-ately categorizing human responsiveness. So, for the cumulative involvement of the socially-produced indivi-dual with his culture-steeped environment, we will use Justus Buchler's notion of "proceiving" as a basis for reconceptualizing what has been misdescribed under such headings as "experience," "sensation," "intellection,"

2

or "perception" (TGT 1951, 2 ed. 1979). By proception is meant the cumulative process of the human individual's assimilation and manipulation of the natural complexes in his or her world.

In its analytic phase, then, philosophic historiography seeks to be philosophic, namely, doubly reflective. In its reconstructive phase it belongs with the sociohistorical sciences (in Aristotle's sense of arts-and-sciences which are technes). And because its proper subject-matter is the distinctively human activities, it is in this special sense a human science. Thus, it is both reflective and self-reflective; and it is both sociohistorical and human query.

This means that philosophy of history functions like a special science, namely, it is required to be assertive, only in its reconstructive phases. In its other phases it will consist either of foundational query, working at uncovering assumptions and consequences, or else it will be an evaluative, critical or creative discourse about its subject-matter. [My essays "Cultural Analysis and Interpretation in the Human Sciences," Man and World XII, 2 (1979), and "The Human Sciences in Dewey, Foucault and Buchler," Southern Journal of Philosophy XVIII, 2 (1980) spell this out more fully.]

Like the discourse of history or philosophy, historiographic discourse may not always be at once explicit about what it is encompassing. As with all literature--and as with Nietzsche's poetic prose or Herakleitos's rhythmic aphorisms or Plato's artfully constructed dialogues, philosophic discourse may choose to be appraisive in the exhibitive mode. What is meant by the "exhibitive mode" (Buchler's term), with and beyond the examples just given, will be explained as we proceed with our account of the conceptions and practice of history among some recent philosophers in the classic American tradition.

William James's Individualist Approach to the Human Process

William James, as we know from a letter to F.C.S. Schiller in 1903 (TCWJ, 1935), gave a delighted reception to the socially oriented work in philosophy and psychology which was being done by what he then called the "Chicago School of Thought." But on himself as a psychologist and on his conception of the social relations of philosophy, the relevant work of John Dewey seems to have had no deep effect--though it may well have reinforced James in some positions he had been developing in theory of knowledge and metaphysics.

While Dewey and G.H. Mead believed that philosophy and psychology are in a relationship to the existential and social matrix of thought which is both immediate and mediatable, as well as reciprocal, James's psychology (experiential as it sought to be) and James's philosophy (voluntaristic as it was) remained to the end individualistic. [Mead's major works, of course, did not appear in time for James--who died in 1910--to read them.] James's psychology and philosophy did transcend the narrow "psychologism," as Santayana called it (STTMP, 1933) of British empiricism, and they did represent an anti-dualistic kind of interactionism and functionalism. But James's psychology falls short of making explicit the social component of experience. James's _Principles of Psychology_ (1890) did recognize the existence of a "social self" which is much akin to the Freudian super-ego and which is a constituent of the total self. But this is not the same as a recognition that the self as a whole is a social product. James's philosophy cannot be made to yield, like Dewey's and Mead's, the outlines of a philosophic sociology of knowledge. And while many readers find in James's work a sense that human creativity is a condition of the social process and a requirement of man's survival, the assumption is not spelled out by James himself.

Given some misconceptions about Dewey as psychologistic, we digress to note that when, early in his philosophic career, Dewey said that psychology could be taken "as the method of philosophy" (PS, PPM 1886) he was saying something different in effect from what his logistical and formalist critics claim he is saying. Dewey was not abstracting, like his critics, from man's sociability or the social givenness of experience (MME 1896). As he says, in another context ten years later,

4

"what ethical theory now needs is an adequate psychological and social method, not a metaphysical one" ("The Metaphysical Method in Ethics," _Psychological Review_ III, _Early Works_, Vol. 5). In making these statements, Dewey was being pragmatist rather than psychologistic. As a matter of focus, of what the subject-matter of philosophic inquiry should be, Dewey was being (as we can now say) "experiential" rather than "empiricist."

Now, though James himself never fully defined the precise places where philosophy, as foundational query, most needs to be applied, some of these places, such as religious experience, were areas of practice and culture which stimulated him to his explicit pursuit of [philosophy as] clarity of thought. James was not trying to rethink the processes of art or culture, but he was a pluralistic and democratic believer in the open society. Why did his pioneering in psychology, metaphysics and theory of knowledge never go beyond a creative kind of individualism?

A biographical and a historical hypothesis suggest themselves in answer to this question. James may have feared all groups as being potentially _totalities_. Contemporary work on the psychology of groups (LI 1890, LS 1895; MM 1897, SC 1901; DLS 1893, RSM 1895; CC 1893, PS 1898) may have supported an individualist fear of the coerciveness or implicit totalitarianism of groups in society and of society itself. Confirmation of this suggestion would be a basis for saying that, had James ever worked to express a social philosophy, he might well have anticipated the insights of Camus, Sartre and Horkheimer about the need for "creative rebellion" and the futility of "totalitarian revolutions." This is not speculative or anachronistic. It seems clear that, in bringing the laboratory techniques of physiological psychology from Wundt's Germany to Boston, James dropped the associated habit of philosophizing in terms of sociohistorical wholes to which Hegel had oriented German thought. The new work in crowd psychology would have reinforced his avoidance of this aspect of Hegelianism [see _A Pluralistic Universe_, Lectures III and V]. Of course, James may simply not have been interested in the analysis of sociohistorical wholes at a philosophic level.

A second hypothesis about why James was not more interested in philosophizing about thought as a social process or about social processes as constitutive of thought, would emphasize the particular tradition of spiritual inwardness within which he was raised as his father's son. This tradition expressed itself, in himself and his literary brother Henry, in the secular form of richly individual and intellectually interesting, intense inner lives. They were both good observers, in their own ways, of what they were interested in; but the combination of American meliorism and provinciality with their types of individual spirituality, seems to have limited or predefined what they could be interested in.

Thus, what we find so well observed in Henry's novels is the delicate interior monologue or perceptivity, just short of traumatic, which grows out the social interactions of individuals in pursuit of an identity, an interest or moral value. In _The Turn of the Screw_ (1898) for instance, Henry documents what happens when the interior monologue and private perception of a hysteric phantasist are exteriorized and imposed upon a social situation which, by definition, she dominates.

What do we find equally well-observed, in a different mode, by William? Where James's German associates and American colleagues in the psychological laboratories of the day were really doing animal psychology, James can be seen to have been investigating in his _Principles of Psychology_ (1890) and _The Varieties of Religious Experience_ (1902) the physiological correlates and psychosomatic conditions of the psychic life of the individual of heightened sensibility or irritability. James was certainly not dealing with the anaesthetized, passive or alienated subject that was to become the implicit paradigm in the behavioral psychologies of J.B. Watson and B.F. Skinner. James's work always granted to the functioning individual that fullness of psychic activity and productivity of images, moods, desires, feelings, thoughts and perceptual combinations which is so neglected by English-language empiricism and behaviorism. Still, to deal only with the physiological psychology and preconscious of the individual or with a variety of isolated spiritual case-histories diagnostically observed, is, nonetheless to abstract from operative social factors.

Thus it is William James who seems to share J.S. Mill's conception of society as only an aggregate of individuals morally responsible to each other. Dewey, in contrast, always thought of the individual as a social product, while not forgetting that society and

6

individual are constitutive of each other. In this connection, with his sense that society and its tendentious institutions are a necessary condition of interesting individuality, Henry was in advance of his brother William. Perhaps William's pragmatic (and Herakleitean) insistence that it is conflict that breeds thought and initiative, can be counted as a step towards this insight; for, conflict presupposes social interaction. The trouble is that with William interaction was too much an affair of only two terms, even when James saw that interactions are always <u>reciprocal</u>. This, however, could be taken positively as a partial anticipation of Dewey's conception of "transactionism" in behavior.

Though James did not insist that the individual's activities are socioculturally informed, his epistemology did provide an analysis of the relation between thought and action which sees the latter as always responsive. "All action," he says in <u>The Will To Believe</u> (WB 1897, or EFM p. 114), is thus re-action upon the outer world." This perception overlaps with Justus Buchler's. Buchler points out, in alluding to Russell's conception of "impulse and desire," that "activity...ordinarily...ascribed to a positive impulse is often better interpreted as a response than as a drive....For the most part, `activity' is best regarded as drawn from the individual rather than as contributed by him" (TGT 1951, p. 61).

Because James's analysis of human activity deals with a "re- agent" or "respondent" rather than a "knower" we can see where, in N. American philosophy, it began to be possible to drop the cognitivistic assumption of both idealism and empiricism. Knowing no longer appeared, in James's pragmatism, to be so unique: "there would appear to be nothing especially unique about the processes of knowing" (MT 1909, p. 142). Four decades after <u>The Meaning of Truth</u> Dewey and Bentley's <u>Knowing and the Known</u> (1949) was to prescind entirely with the "knower" and to identify "knowings" with the "knowns" in the adaptive transactions which it set out to analyze afresh. Nor does knowing seem, in James's analysis, to be psychological man's main way of relating to the environment or, even, to be the main component in experience.

"Experience," Action and "Judgment"

As pragmatists, James and Dewey were indeed seeking to rescue "experience" from its impoverishment by British empiricism and its over-intellectualization by idealism. In retrospect, the historian can now say--with Buchler, who said it first--that most philosophers "have been concerned with experience mainly in so far as it bears upon 'knowlege'....They have inadvertently left it to art to deal with experience in its proper breadth and to render exhibitively what they should equally have recognized and encompassed assertively" (NJ 1955, p.141).

The pragmatists' attempt to broaden the reference of the conception of experience, however, retained much of the cognitivist emphasis in some new forms. James's concern with the primacy, depth and richness of experience became, in Dewey, mainly a concern with it as intelligent, or problem-solving, action. In reconstructing the empiricist notion of experience as a passive process, Dewey saw it as "an affair primarily of doing" (RP 1920, p. 82) and as "active and planning thought within the very process of experience" (ib. p. 89). Notice how the latter quotation singles out thought from the experiential matrix or continuum.

In bringing experience home from the transcendental realms of idealism Dewey made it, more than a matter of action, a matter of more or less conscious instrumental striving. "Every existence is an experiment in fact, even though not in design," he says in _Experience and Nature_ (1925, p. 69). He thought of experience in "its vital form" as primarily "experimental, an effort to change the given," a search for control over the environment ("The Need for a Recovery in Philosophy," repr. Vol. 10 _The Middle Works_). While this may be true to the experience of the practising artist, scientist or statesman, it is not true of social or private life in general. While it may be the case that a dianoetically active individual processes his impressions in such a way as to be habitually prepared for successful action, others habitually seek only understanding or some other kind of security from their involvements. To say further, as Dewey does in _Reconstruction in Philosophy_ (1920, p. 83), that "disconnected doing and disconnected suffering are neither of them experience" excludes too much from experience. Dewey, as Buchler notes (TGT 2 ed. Introduction), also makes a twofold assumption that "what happens to an individual cannot

8

be part of his experience unless it stems from his own action" and "unless he is aware of it." This not only excludes too much; it leaves, for Buchler and other readers, too many "explanatory gaps" in an account of the human process.

It is these gaps that Buchler's work in systematic philosophy has sought to supply. They remained in Dewey's work in spite of Dewey's existential emphasis on the biological and social matrix of human activity, and in spite of his new analysis of "inquiry." --He had substituted this term for the term "reflective thinking" in Logic: The Theory of Inquiry (1938).-- While he had enriched the conception of experience with his notion of "the consummatory," in his analysis of art of 1934 (Art as Experience), he did not free "experience" from his equation of it with the organization of experience and with consciousness. And he failed to see that works of art also constitute judgments in another mode than inquiry does.--This is the mode that Buchler calls "the exhibitive mode" of judgment.--And whether it is entirely correct or not to say that Dewey made action of "primary" importance in his analysis of the human enterprise (human action or conduct is, after all, the subject-matter of history), he fell short of seeing that what we call conduct also institutes determinacies in reality and, as such, is also judicative in a mode distinct from that of "inquiry." --This is the mode that Buchler calls "the active mode of judgment."

Because the assertive mode is the only mode for Dewey in which judgments can be properly effected, art and conduct to not have intellectual parity with inquiry in Dewey. His interest in practice did not lead him back to Aristotle's insight that reflective practice and reflective construction are also distinct kinds of knowledge, so that art and action have their own irreducible sorts of intelligibility. Nor did Dewey see that human practices as such and human products as such, in instituting determinacy, are also to be taken as judicative if they are not to be pushed beyond the spectrum of activities that can be made intelligible in their own terms and whose effect in the human process cannot be denied.

Dewey, thus, tends to assimilate the exhibitive and the active ways of creating order to the "scientific" way [in a non-Aristotelian sense of "scientific"]. Perceiving that science is "normative," in his carefully explicated sense of the term, Dewey did not hold

9

enough to his sense of science as also "exploratory." This property of inquiry seems to have dissolved into that of the "corrigibility" of hypotheses. But insofar as it is exploratory and interrogative, science can be seen as "query" (Buchler's term), though it is specifically "inquiry" in being falsifiable and verifiable, namely, true or false. In any case, exhibitive and active judgment, which are non-assertive query and not explicit in the propositional sense, are just as pervasive and fundamental to the human process as assertive judgment. As for the interrogative and appraisive process out of which works of history arise, and the scientific and rhetorical process within which they are constructed, a moment's reflection tells us that history is query, in that it is an active, constructive or exhibitive effort as well as a scientific and assertive one.

While William James's most perceptive expounders have also noted that he abstracted, in his academic works, from the formative power of the social matrix of experience this is not the whole story (PSCWJ 1980). In his essay on "The Promethean Self and Community in the Philosophy of William James," J. McDermott qualifies this recognition positively by bringing out the striking compatibility between James's view of the self as transactionally creative (and self-creative), and the existentialist views of Nietzsche and Sartre about the self. James believed that history would always end by vindicating the individual against the group (Letters, 1920; vol. II, p.90). For him, as for Aristotle, consciousness was not a substance but an activity. And the subject, for James, is identical with the whole interacting organism, as in Buchler's account of proception [see below, ch. 6].

Conation, or willing, is cognitive for James; but the ego is not transcendental. To choose an interpretation of the world is to have a self and secure it from its Protean vulnerability (WWJ, p. 7f.). For the self, to be is to be in place, to be somewhere (ERE, p. 86n.); the body locates us by supplying coordinates and supporting the experience of relations which is the self. But so is community, according to McDermott, the ramified experience of relations. The self in James is fragile but it is aggressive, namely, it is functional. With its Jamesian "halo of relations" or "penumbra" it personalizes everything, including especially the social (common) ingredients of experience. In other words, just because individual responses are relation-saturated (McDermott's term) subjectivity is not only possible but saves us from the banal domination of the common, stylizing it or modifying it in some novel way.

It is therefore no surprise to find James being colloquially explicit, in his letters, about the debt an individual's thought owes to the acts of others and about the man-made nature of our form of life (Letters I, p. 130f.). J. Barzun has pointed this out again, recently, in his A Stroll with William James (1983, p.17). Barzun also quotes from James's Memories and Studies the apposite passage about history in which we too will take delight: "You can give humanistic value to almost anything by teaching it historically. Geology, economics, mechanics are humanities when taught with reference to the successive achievements of the geniuses to which these sciences owe their being. Not taught thus, literature remains grammar, art a catalogue, history a list of dates, and natural science a sheet of formulas and weights and measures. The sifting of human creations!--nothing less than this is what we ought to mean by the humanities."

Bibliography

NE Aristotle Nicomachean Ethics, ed. & tr. H. Rackham (Loeb Libr. 1934)

PA Aristotle Parts of Animals, ed. & tr. A.L. Peck (Loeb Libr. 1945)

PS 1886. J. Dewey "The Psychological Standpoint," Mind XI, and
PPM " "Psychology as Philosophic Method," Mind XI, The Early Works Vol. 1, ed. Bowers and Boydston (Carbondale: S. Illinois Univ. Press 1969)

PP 1890. W. James The Principles of Psychology 2 vols. (New York: Holt 1890)

LLI 1890. G. Tarde Les Lois de l'Imitation (Paris: Alcan 1890)

LFC 1892. S. Sighele La Foule Criminelle (Paris: Alcan 1892)

LCC 1893. S. Sighele La Coppia Criminale (Torino: Bocca; 2 ed. 1897)

DLS 1893. E. Durkheim The Division of Labor in Society (Glencoe: Free Press 1933; 1 ed. Paris: Alcan 1893)

LLS 1895. G. Tarde La Logique Sociale (Paris: Alcan 1895)

PF 1895. G. Le Bon Psychologie des Foules (Paris: Alcan; trans. N.Y. Macmillan 1896, The Crowd)

RSM 1895. E. Durkheim Les Regles de la Methode Sociologique; trans. Rules of Sociological Method (Free Press 1964)

MME 1896. J. Dewey "The Metaphysical Method in Ethics," Psychological Review III; Early Works Vol. 5

MM 1897. E.A. Ross "Mob Mind," Popular Science, Vol. 51 (1897)

WB 1897. W. James The Will To Believe (New York:

Longmans 1897)

TS 1898. H. James _The Turn of the Screw_ (New York: Macmillan 1898)

PDS 1898. S. Sighele _Psychologie des Sectes_ (Paris: Girard 1898)

SC 1901. E.A. Ross _Social Control_ (New York: Macmillan); restates works of the 1890's publ. in _The American Journal of Sociology_.

OF 1901. G. Tarde _L'Opinion et la Foule_ (Paris: Alcan 1901)

VRE 1902. W. James _The Varieties of Religious Experience_ (London: Longmans 1902)

APU 1909. W. James _A Pluralistic Universe_ (N.Y. Longmans 1909)

MT 1909. W. James _The Meaning of Truth_ (N.Y. Longmans 1909)

MS 1911. W. James _Memories and Studies_ (N.Y. Longmans; repr. 1941 and 1971)

ERE 1912. W. James _Essays in Radical Empiricism_ (N.Y. Longmans)

NRP 1917. J. Dewey "The Need for a Recovery in Philosophy," repr. in _The Middle Works_ Vol. 10 (Carbondale: S. Illinois U.P. 1980)

LTRS 1920 _The Letters of William James_ 2 vols. ed. H. James (Boston: Atlantic 1920)

RP 1920 J. Dewey _Reconstruction in Philosophy_ (N.Y. Holt 1920)

EN 1925 J. Dewey _Experience and Nature_ (Chicago: Open Court), _The Later Works_ Vol. 1 (Carbondale: S. Illinois U.P. 1981)

AE 1934 J. Dewey _Art as Experience_ (N.Y. Minton Balch 1934)

TCWJ 1935 R.B. Perry _The Thought and Character of_

               William James (Boston: Little Brown 1935)

STTMP 1937. G. Santayana Some Turns of Thought in Modern Philosophy (N.Y. Scribner's), Triton ed. Vol. VII. STTMP contains papers from 1923-1932.

LTI 1938 J. Dewey Logic: The Theory of Inquiry (N.Y. Holt 1938)

KK 1949 J. Dewey & A. Bentley Knowing and the Known (Boston: Beacon 1949)

TGT 1951 J. Buchler Toward a General Theory of Human Judgment (N.Y. Columbia; 2 ed. w. Intro. Dover 1979)

NJ 1955 J. Buchler Nature and Judgment (N.Y. Columbia; repr. by Grosset & Dunlap 1966)

FHK 1965 M. White Foundations of Historical Knowledge (N.Y. Harper & Row 1965)

APH 1965 A. Danto Analytical Philosophy of History (Cambridge: the University Press 1965)

WWJ 1967 J. McDermott, ed. The Writings of William James (N.Y. Random House 1967)

OKHP 1973 M. Murphey Our Knowledge of the Historical Past (N.Y. Bobbs-Merrill 1973)

CAIHS 1979 V. Tejera "Cultural Analysis and Interpretation in the Human Sciences," Man and World XII, No.2 (1979)

HSDFB 1980 V. Tejera "The Human Sciences in Dewey, Foucault and Buchler," Southern Journal of Philosophy XVIII, 2

PSCWJ 1980 J. McDermott "The Promethean Self and Community in the Philosophy of William James," Rice University Studies 66, No. 4 (1980)

SWWJ 1983 J. Barzun A Stroll With William James (N.Y. Harper and Row)

Chapter II

Retrospect on the State of the Question

The Epistemological Approach to History

While N. American philosophy from Woodbridge and Santayana to Lamprecht and Randall has been characteristically sensitive to the nature of history and to its implications for philosophic activity as interrogation, interpretation and vision (PH 1916, RM 1926; LR 1905-06; MN 1929-66; MM 1925, 1940, NHE 1958, HPUP 1963, CP 1962-77), transatlantic philosophy of history in the post World War II Analytic style was, as we have said, simply epistemological. Because the debate in the Analytic style was centered on the special-science conception that what history should do is "explain" in the nomological-deductive sense of "explain," the terms in which the debate was conducted were necessarily, and unnoticedly, anti-historical. And there was as little communication on the subject of history between the classic American tradition and the Analytic style as there was between the Analytic tradition and the historians themselves.

In a longer retrospect, it seems ironic that so much of the historical movement of the Nineteenth century, including especially the Rankeians (ZKNG 1824, VH) became, in spite of Hegel, anti-philosophical. A century later, as if one extreme could redress another, recent Analytic philosophy of history has emerged as anti-historical both in its demands upon history and in its attitudes to the history of thought and philosophy. Just as early Twentieth century American historians and thinkers could object to law-seeking, synthetic philosophies of history such as Spengler's (UA 1918-22, DW 1926-28) as pseudo-scientific, so can present-day American critics object to the claims of recent Analytic philosophy of history as scientistic and reductive.

The problem is that the latter assumes that the concern of histories is with laws of change or laws of occurrence, and that historical explanations of events must be like explanations in the most exact natural sciences. But where, in the synthetic philosophies of history, the notion of explanation remained unexplicated, "explanation" in Analytic philosophy of history has been both over-extended and become too narrow to correspond to the processes of explanation in fact

15

employed by competent historians.

Analytic philosophy of history thinks it has entirely abandoned Comte's speculative doctrine of the
three stages of human development which led to the
triumph of science over theology. But one difficulty in
Analytic philosophy of history is just the positivist
inheritance which has kept it in a state of unnoticed
antithesis and agreement with the old theology that
down-graded human nature. Though positivism sometimes
appeared to be a kind of humanism because it was nat-
ure-centered rather than God-oriented, it failed to
develop a conception of the human or social sciences
that gives to these any philosophic significance or
foundational function in the pursuit of knowledge. Just
as positivism's lack of concern for human nature is
hidden from itself by its unquestioning optimism; so,
positivist philosophers of science have failed to take
the human as a subject for observation.

They take this subject so for granted in the
observation of nature that the human observer is left
out of the account. In positivist philosophy of science, the nature being observed is something which does
not include human nature as a part of it. As a philosophy positivism has not, in this respect, progressed
beyond the old theology which physical science displaced. For, just as the old theology accounted for man
in terms of a God of which man was not constitutive;
so, scientistic positivism, when it discusses how to
account for man, prescribes that man must be understood
in terms of a nature of which man is not constitutive.

A.J. Ayer in his Auguste Comte Memorial Lecture of
1964 (MSS), while insisting on the continuity of the
social and the physical--much as pragmatism always
has--still fails to see that the physical is not more
"primary" than any other dimension, except in some
order of postulation. The difference, in Dewey and
pragmatism generally, is that the social and the human
are not taken to be derivative from the physical, even
though the social, the human and the physical are not
discontinuous with each other.

It is worth noting that Comte, the founder of
Positivism, was a susceptible admirer of the analytical
mechanics of J.L. Lagrange (MA 1788, 1815) in a way
similar to that in which, a hundred years later, the
Vienna positivists were to be influenced by the mechan-
istic physics of E. Mach. Einstein himself, while pay-

16

ing tribute to Mach's antidogmatism in science, repudiated his epistemology ("Autobiographical Notes," AEPS 1951). To go back to the beginning: John Locke, the "father of epistemology," claimed in an ironic confession to have written his Essay under the stimulus of Newton's Principia, or mathematical principles of celestial mechanics. Locke, however, had been working since 1671 (LLJL 1829) on the problems treated by his Essay (ECHU 1690, EDLE 1936). Locke's reflection in the Essay is more critical of Newton and the "masterbuilders" in physical science than is usually realized. Read carefully, he can be seen to be troubled by the vagueness of some of Newton's key concepts, and skeptical of the way they are embedded in a hugely impressive mathematical system which has the effect of protecting them from criticism (PMPN 1686). Non-English readers of Locke's Augustan prose are more excusable for missing the point than are English speakers. The misunderstanding is partly cause and partly effect of the trend towards physicalism that had begun to assert itself in the Seventeenth century.

Von Ranke the historian, though often invoked by the later positivists, was not himself one (GRGV 1824, TPH). [The famous Preface to the Geschichten der Romanischen und Germanischen Voelker, published in 1824, is missing from G.R. Dennis's English translation. It can be found in F. Stern's Varieties of History. The attack on Fichte is in a fragment dated 1830, also to be found in VH.] It was simply that he repudiated any kind of a priori or speculative laws about the development of mankind. Von Ranke's strictures, for instance, against Fichte's assumption of a world plan of five epochs are so generally worded as an attack against all philosophic denials of the contingencies of history, that it would be a contradiction to exempt Comte's schemes about progress (SPP 1824 and 1851-54, CPSS 1825, CPP 1830-42, CPS 1853) from these strictures. The same applies to those social-science "laws" which are repeatedly desiderated but seldom produced by speculative historians like Teggart (PH 1918, TH 1925) or logical positivists like Hempel (FGLH 1942). Contrary to von Ranke's view, such laws would make historical events deducible and turn them into instances of abstractions.

In particular, and in connection with the historical development of physical science, it is a mistake to seek accounts or reconstructions that are nomological, i.e. derivable from given laws. This kind of history of science tries to discover the "logical structure of the development" of the science. That is, it assumes that there are laws of development in this part of intellectual history. Thus, while sometimes repudiating speculative philosophies of general history, the deductivist historian of physics often remains in practice a speculative philosopher of scientific history. In fact, the actual historical development of physical science has been more a matter of trial and error, more tortuous and polemical than can possibly appear from a logical account of it. The contrast with Comte should be documented: "No conception," he said, "can be understood except through its history" (CPP 1830-42, Ch. 1). The reduction of a historical account to a logical structure denies the temporal element in the process [as we shall see below]. The history of a theoretical enterprise does not itself have a theoretical form, even when it is possible, in retrospect and in the abstract, to present later stages of the theory as a deductive consequence of the earlier.

Now, one of the results of the epistemological approach has been to displace into accounts of the art-and-science of history a requirement of scientific discourse in the deductive sciences, namely, that of logical consistency. But the existence of philosophic works not in the assertive mode, such as Plato's _Meno_ or _Theaetetus_, which are constructions with epistemological themes successfully meeting rhetorical and literary criteria of effective communication, shows that clarity _about_ the pursuit of knowledge can be achieved by other means than assertion, and independently of logical consistency. By implication, the epistemological approach also imposes this requirement upon histories themselves in a too strict and wholesale way.

To isolate what, on the basis of its borrowed paradigm, epistemology calls "the knowledge-element" in histories, and dissmissively to assign all the other elements to "the literary phases" of histories (FHK p. 220f.), is to separate the art of a history too sharply from "the discipline which aims to discover and order the truth"--as if the literary art of a history was not also a discipline and had no share in communicating "the truth." It is also to commit the common fallacy of sundering form from content in communicative interactions. It leaves unmonitored the effect that _the way in which_ a thing is said has upon the reader and upon what is said. And it is blind to the communicative effect, what Buchler calls the exhibitive judgment, enacted by the very order or shape itself of what is being offered as history.

Readers of histories will have noticed the contrast between the richness of historical discourse in its varieties, and the putatively unambiguous discourse of the deductive sciences from which epistemology derives its model of knowledge. The language of histories is as often expressive and informative as it is assertive or informational. The appraisive language of narrative history is not only the matrix for the social-science types of claim histories make, this language is constitutive of the constructions we call histories.

A historian's discourse is a necessary condition of history in a way that an experimental scientist's is not, by itself, generative of his published results. The historian does more than use language as his medium, but his final product must be a readable discourse. This discourse will not only have an exhibitive dimension, such as even statistical tables have, it will be a synthesis of a set of claims made in the assertive mode with a set of values held implicitly and suggestions not made assertively. This is not to say that history is query because it is only exhibitive and works in non-assertive ways. Histories are also inquiry and assertive. They are, in fact, bi-modal. A historian both uses or practices a number of special sciences (such as demography, archaeology or economics) and practices or uses, whether consciously or not, rhetorical and literary (presentational) techniques.

Narrative and Nomology I

Our subject, however, is not histories themselves but the philosophy of history in recent times. In the broader picture, the epistemological style whose philosophy of history I am criticizing, was not only a reaction against the generally idealist "speculative metaphysics" of the Nineteenth and early Twentieth centuries, it was also inimical to the kind of humanist and naturalist analysis practiced--in what became the American tradition--by John Dewey and George Santayana. The animosity, it now appears, was directed not so much at their systematic bent as against their non-logistical way of being systematic. Aware as they both were of the cultural involvement and existential matrix of philosophy, Santayana's pursuit of fullness of understanding was more historical in orientation while Dewey's was habitually more biological and sociological in its concerns. The former chose to philosophize in the literary mold of the great topical and contemplative essayists, the latter in an idiom akin to the discourse of the modern social sciences.

We need to recognize that philosophic activity in general can be practiced in different modes. The nucleus of three modes of judgment which Buchler has distinguished and validated in his systematic work (TGT, NJ, CM, MNC, OCW, PIN) will be used by this monograph in telling its story, and to help articulate the ideas about history which are its subject. I should make it clear here that this is a study of an aspect of the N. American tradition from within that tradition, and that this study uses the terms developed by Buchler to criticize the whole Western tradition of construing the notion of judgment. It also uses terms, distinctions and insights derived from a naturalist and humanist reading of the original (non-Neoclassicist, non-Scholastic) Aristotle and from a dialogical reading of the original (non-Neoplatonist, non-assertive) works of Plato.

The philosophic appraisal of beliefs, when practiced in the exhibitive mode, as it was by Plato in his dialogues, is one kind of query. When, as has been more usual, it is practiced in the assertive mode it is another kind of query, namely, inquiry. In contrast to epistemology, which is reflection about knowledge after the fact of knowledge, metaphysics has come to be thought of as the inescapable byproduct of every pursuit of knowledge; for, every pursuit of knowledge or claim to it generates implications about what there is. But "metaphysics" as systematic philosophy, as the art and science of getting control of this inevitable output, far from being the disorder epistemologists once said it was, can provide another kind of check upon theory of knowledge than that provided by inspection of the cases of knowledge which are the subject-matter of the latter.

Metaphysics the discipline has a systematic responsibility not just to practice conceptual analysis but to be ready to re-examine and improve upon the terms and categories used by analysis and which, in escaping analysis themselves, have systemic effects. Here, the complacent notion that the activity of "doing" philosophy is more important than its practice in writing, may have militated against this kind of systematic critique and clarification of the concepts used by conceptual analysis. On our approach, philosophy of history will also have to be historiography in the sense of the aesthetics of history, the study of the making of histories.

This makes it difficult to grasp A. Danto's drastic statement (NYRB 23-2-67, p. 14) that the philosophy of history he was doing in his Analytic Philosophy of History has as little interest for historians as the epistemological discussion of the existence of material objects would have for physical scientists. If this is the case, then the author misrepresents the nature of his book in calling it "philosophy of history." By calling it this nonetheless, Danto is conceding that it would be alright pari passu to call epistemology the "philosophy of physics." Now, to restrict Analytic philosophy to epistemology is a stipulation that must be left for Analysts themselves to make. But what sort of application of philosophy to its subject is one which makes no contact with it? Can we even call it an exercise in "applied logic," as Analytic philosophy sometimes defines itself, if it is irrelevant to the practice of history? To be relevant would not reflection have to go beyond this kind of epistemology and reflect upon histories, not in terms of logic alone but in terms of what historians, archaeologists, philologists, social scientists and cultural critics do as historians, and in terms of what general historians do with the special sciences?

But this is not what Danto's book does. He attempts, for instance, to improve upon and correct Ch. Beard's statement of historical relativism or C. Hempel's nomothetic-deductive model of explanation (APH p.206ff. and 88ff.) without abandoning his epistemological strategy of assimilating the procedures and products of history to the paradigms previously worked out for natural science by logical positivists and logical Analysts. He never thinks to question the assumptions at the basis of these paradigms and their transferability to non-nomothetic, non-mathematical sciences. As he says, "no amount of historical competence especially qualifies a man to do philosophy of history, for the latter is an exercise of philosophical, not historical techniques" (loc. cit.).

But Danto has not used the philosophical techniques which are aimed at uncovering operative or unnoticed assumptions and analogies, or which aim at freeing observation from conceptual blinkers, as in C.S. Peirce's cenoscopy (CP 8.199, 8.201f.). [It is of historical interest that Peirce gives so much credit, in these paragraphs, to Wundt for his development of "cenoscopy." The term, according to Peirce, was invented by Bentham.] Nor has Danto used techniques which seek to insure that the distinctions being made are germane, not external to the subject-matter under observation.

A thinker who wants a subject-matter to be responsive to his distinctions will have to make himself responsible for that subject-matter in itself and as it relates to other inquires and interests. One cannot be responsibly cross-disciplinary by subtly or peremptorily imposing on other disciplines the structure of his own favorite discipline. There is nothing sovereign about epistemology that can legitimate its imposition upon the arts and sciences of the values and structure of the physical science from which, as a second-order inquiry, it derives. The more so, when it does not include an interest in keeping control of the ontological outputs or priority-creating inputs of specific inquiries and products. To rephrase Danto, no amount of "philosophical" competence especially qualifies a person to do philosophy of history unless his analyses are responsive to the techniques and nature of history.

Another way of describing what Analytic epistemology (as represented by Hempel, White, Danto, and Murphey's OKHP) has been doing, is to say that it has tried to describe what histories would have to be like if history were a theoretical science of the same sort as the sciences from which epistemology is derived. To do this Danto's epistemology has conceptualized stories as being "narrative explanations." Next, it conceives of "narrative explanations" as consisting of "sequences of narrative sentences." Thirdly, it believes that these sentences express or imply <u>causal</u> linkages between or within themselves. Lastly, it postulates (i) that every such causal linkage gets its efficacy from a possible general law which guarantees the connection, and (ii) that these general laws are <u>somehow</u> <u>present</u> in the narrative explanations even though historians almost never state them.

Danto's model of what happens in historical discourse is patterned, with variations, on Hempel's nomothetic-deductive model of the nature of explanation in the natural sciences (FGLH 1942). A basic question about this model is whether it is actually the best available, when account is taken of all the natural sciences as well as the social sciences. How serviceable is Hempel's model in highly empirical areas of the science and practice of medicine, or in such contingency-ridden sciences as anthropology or historical semantics? Given that general laws in these sciences are either so highly qualified and nominal, or truistic or non-existent, is it not misconceived to refer the sense that something has has been explained to the possibility of its subsumption as a particular under a general law?

In the assumed parallel between the natural sciences and history there are two basic equivocations in the use of the terms "explain" and "cause." There is a strategic confusion in the appeal to Hempel's model which fails to distinguish the specific senses in which history <u>is</u> a science (a practical and productive science, as Aristotle would say) and the sense in which it <u>uses</u> special sciences such as statistics or economics. There is also an equivocation between what we can call the "circumstantial antecedents" of an event and the invariable antecedents which they must be proved to be, before they can be taken as "causal."

What we get from referring a particular event to a general law, as its explanation, is the reassurance that a scientifically familiar pattern or natural process has prevailed. But the <u>proposition</u> that the invariant structure of the process is universal in its prevalence, is non-existential as the logicians say. As we know, the universal proposition whether categorical or hypothetical is non-existential because it is purely definitional or relational. Thus, we can be only postulationally committed to the invariant pattern. Its function is just to reassert the orderliness of nature in our attempts to get control over its dynamic processes. It is possible that another invariant pattern can be formulated which will serve this purpose more effectively; but it will be equally "non-existential" when asserted as a universal proposition. This means that the determining criterion, in the history of scientific choice among theories, has been the pragmaticist one of intellectual economy and serviceability in experience.

Whatever the theoretical or technological fate of such universal claims about invariance, the sense they give that something has been "explained" derives from the strategy of referring the singular, the less familiar, the novel to what has become familiar as a generalization. The convenient familiarity of the generalization makes us forget its non-existential and hypothetical character. Nonetheless, the feeling that something has been explained by ivocation of the expected, while real in one sense, is illusory and weak in another. For, we must also notice that there has really been no "explanation," only fulfillment of a prophetic universal or general law. Explanation would be called for, would be really needed only if the general law was broken or denied by a surprising instance that it had failed to predict! This phenomenon, because of its contrast with literary narrative, calls for a short digression on the latter.

Among the many ways in which stories function, they often give a feeling that something has been "explained." But in stories and historical narratives the source of the feeling is quite other than in natural science. In narrative, unfamiliar behaviors, the unknown quantities of character, nonce occurrences and operations, all are respectively described, inferred or connected by suggestion: that is to say, in implicit antithesis with previously expected patterns of behavior, stereotypes or modalities. Were they not connected within this sort of tension the story would not be interesting enough to continue reading. A historical narrative will not be true to the past situation if what was unexpected in it does not remain unexpected to the actors in the narrative. This, or some other kind of suspense must be used to keep the reader's attention. If the historian using demography, psychoanalysis, economics etc. is, in retrospect, able to show that the unexpected need not have been unpredictable to an intelligent agent, this means only that the narrator is now doing social science as a historical agent might have done had he possessed present-day tools.

Here the question obtrudes itself, if a narrative must in fact hold the attention by using or creating suspense, how can the function of narrative be to explain? The business of an interesting narrative is to neutralize predictability, in contrast to a nomological account whose concern is to show that the expected has occurred as expected. Whatever tension there is in reading a nomological account, is external to it and comes from a residual fear that it might not be fulfilled, a fear that nature is not orderly and therefore not controllable or safe.

Completion of a nomological account brings with it a kind of theoretical satisfaction. The tension in reading a story, however, is both generated by the narrative itself and assuaged by it. Because one of the conditions of a good story is that it make contact, at some point and at some level that hurts or excites, with the human condition, the completion of the story also brings with it a feeling of satisfaction. This feeling is continuous with the feelings informed or reordered by valid myth. In either case we have been reinforced in a positive expectation, in the one that the human condition is tolerable, in the other that nature need not be terrifying. What has been "explained" in both cases, quite indirectly and implicitly, is that life is after all worth living or somehow manageable.

The satisfaction, by an instance, of a nomothetic generalization is described as a theoreticist demand because what the instance is taken to confirm is a theory. In an earlier stage of the rise of scientific and scientistic thinking, this procedure was thought of as providing an account of _how_ a thing came to occur. Natural science understood itself to be concerned, in Aristotelian terms, with material conditions and efficient and formal--mathematical or nomothetic-- "causes." It was not concerned with "final" causes or the "why" of phenomena but with the "how." Final causes were rejected outright as supererogatory and non-explanatory. It is therefore surprising to find the scientistic philosophers under review, couching their demands for explanation in history in such formalist terms, in ways which tend to identify formal causes with final causes.

This is germane to the problem of explanation in history because histories are concerned with theories mainly as products, as part of the subject-matter of intellectual history. Most histories do not themselves seek to be theoretical, though a handful--like Comte's or Marx's, Spengler's or Toynbee's--have also offered theories of the occurrence of some of the events they rehearse.

Histories seek, overwhelmingly, to reconstruct the circumstances within which events occurred or historical agents acted, as well as the circumstances which ensued upon given actions. When the "why" of a given action is sought, it is sought by historians in terms of the agents' reasons for their actions--as opposed to the causes of these actions. To ask for the cause of an action or situation is to ask for the relevant economic, psychological, ecological, demographic, etc. determinants of it. It is to ask the historian to become an economist, psychologist, ecologist, etc. Thus the scientistic complaints about the weakness of explanations in histories are not only misplaced; they are really complaints about the difficulties some special sciences have in providing explanations as nomologically satisfactory as those provided by theoretical physics.

Thus, nomothetic-deductive explanation, so far as it is explanation, and narrative accounts, as far as they can be said to explain, are not homologous in the way they work. And in so far as what the first provides is a logical structure and not a temporal deployment like the second, it would seem impossible to conflate them.

Interestingly, as Kenneth Burke suggests (PLF 1941, p.100), Hegel's _dialectic_ _of_ _history_ can be taken as a logic of history that tries to do just this. In a logic, as in a musical chord, only tones that harmonize, only elements that don't contradict each other, can be expressed simultaneously. But if the same chord is stretched out into an arpeggio, discordant ingredients can be introduced and made to sound like passing notes or dismissible elements.--We add that when an _antithetical_ element is juxtaposed, a moment later, to a _thetic_ element and the two are held over (_aufgehoben_) into, or transcended by, a synthesis the resulting synthesis sounds harmonious either because it was preconceived to sound so or because it has dropped what it cannot reconcile.--The richest consonances may contain the most apparent assonances, but contradictory elements sounded at one moment cannot and do not create a harmony. They can be resolved only in a temporally developed context. Burke implies that to avoid making good and evil "consubstantial," Hegel's logic must remain a temporal dialectic, else the whole enterprise "would be over before it started" (PLF p. 99). The characteristic insight behind this, readers of Burke will have guessed, is that any dialectical development is potentially dramatic. And this anticipates what has to be said in this study about the dramatic dimension of both the histories we read and the human past they reconstruct.

The related suggestion that narratives do feature universal claims, can be tested against the universal proposition with which Jane Austen opens _Pride_ _and_ _Prejudice_. "It is a truth universally acknowledged, that a single man of good fortune must be in want of a wife." The proposition is ironically intended. The male protagonist does not believe it. And the author, whose voice we hear in it, can pretend to believe it because the marriageable ladies in the county act as if they believed it. But so far as Jane Austen also sympathizes with her hero she must suspend belief, just as she must because she is the narrator.

What the mock universal proposition does is set the tone with which Austen will share her story with the reader. It could be said to generate the complex point of view from which the story will be told, but it could not be said to generate the story. Were it a nomological universal, it would take only a few sentences to instantiate or deny it. The universal does not subsume the story, but is a dramatized proposition symbolic of the external conditions of the tension which Austen's narrative art is going to develop and resolve. The comic universal, then, is a kind of epigraph that Austen has put at the beginning of her novel to set the tone, to generate dramatic tension, and to challenge her own novelistic power to give interesting value to a careless neoclassical sterotype which is nomologically worthless as a premise of straight social science. This "universal" in literature does not serve to explain anything; it is rather Jane Austen who has found a way of entertainingly explaining it in her novel. A social historian proceeding nomologically would be required, presumably, to show both that the nubile agents in his history (or their managers) were acting on this premise and that, as one of his social science theorems, the proposition was either confirmed or falsified by his documentable observation of county courting-behavior in Eighteenth century England.

As for the modification of Hempel's model, proposed by Danto and others, according to which the general laws required for purposes of explanation are to be supplemented, in historical writing, by the truisms, half-truths or unquestioned assumptions of everyday life--it is not admissible. It commits an equivocation between freefloating asumptions, few of which respectable historians would want to invoke nomologically, and general laws which formulate the results of scientific analysis and are deductively consistent with each other.

It is strange to find "rigorous" philosophers of the exact sciences like Hempel, speaking--in connection with history--of "laws" that can't be stated as laws, or stated "with precision" or "so that they are in agreement with all the relevant empirical evidence available" (FGLH). If a law cannot be formulated so as to cover all the relevant empirical evidence available, then it is not a law for the occurrence of the instances in question. Here epistemologists are only acting as if there were such a law. And they are not acting as if there could be one at a later stage of inquiry, since they admit that at best the formulations which do the work of general laws in history are trite or truistic, partial or inane or incompletely verified (APH p. 243). Just as basically, Hempel's model and its

28

modifications cannot be an account of the nature of narrative because they all abstract from the flow of time. The nomothetic-deductive model uses the purely conceptual device of the _instant_, in order to specify different _states_ which are themselves abstractions from or cuts in the continuum of time. But the instant is a negation of time which conceptually arrests this continuum. Correspondingly, in the literary dimension, there is no way of registering what is called a timeless instant except by resort to the enlargement or delaying of it in slow motion.

When, after careful study, Ernest Nagel concludes that _collective_ events of any complexity are not explained by subsuming them as single units under abstract concepts appearing in generalizations (SS 1961, p. 574), and that "historical explanations [in the nomological sense] of individual actions are...probabilistic in structure, their form being the outcome of the...statistical character of the available generalizations that enter into explanatory assumptions," we can fairly say that the deductive model has been found minimally applicable to the practice of history by the nomothetic-deductive model itself.

And because "explanations of aggregative events are constituted out of strands of subordinate accounts whose patterns are those of _probabilistic_ and _genetic_ explanations" (SS 574, my emphasis), we have to say that satisfying the nomological form of explanation either does not serve to warrant the conclusions logically--since "probabilistic" means that the conclusions are not necessary consequences of their premises--or that their warrant lies in the genetic nature or derivation of the premises.

This in turn is, again, a matter of the plausibility of the tacit relatability silently binding the particular events cited in the narrative sequence, and the security with which the historian has established their sequence and particular occurrence. It is thus, after all, the quality of the historian's reflection about the probable and the care with which he has treated and selected the particulars which give the historian's account its creditibility. But these are just the characteristics that make history a practical or productive science and unsuited to nomologization.

Analysis of a situation, we were saying, in abstraction from the time factor or time sequence would not be history, but political science or military science or economics, etc. in the nomological sense of science. On the other hand, narrative "explanations" which ignored laterally contemporaneous events would be unable to narrate how the compresence or conflict of separate agencies came to concur at a given time, or how initially isolated clusters of factors destined to come together in time, moved from their isolation into a pattern of dynamic interaction with resultants. As historical questions, the analytic question "what were the components of the situation" and the narrative question "how did this situation arise," are inseparable in practice though distinguishable in thought.

We can restate the matter by saying that the historian in fact asks "how did these components come to constitute this situation, what came to be the stakes, what was emerging as dependent on the outcome, and on what was the outcome coming to depend?" These are both analytic and narrative questions. Narrative accounts become analytical in histories mainly as a result of the rhetorical turn called "point of view": it distances the author from the drama he has been unfolding and allows him to arrest developments for the sake of comment (as in story-telling) or analysis (as in social history or criticism). The point of view then changes from being internal to the narrative, from within the situation of the actors or agencies, to being external and either nomological, ethical or historiographic. There is an unavoidable change, mild or massive, in mode of understanding from what can be called the sympathetic or dramatic to the ironic or detached.

This does not mean that, in switching from historical narration to nomological analysis or social criticism, the historian always intends to be ironic or deliberately appeals to a rhetorical device. It simply means that the literary trope called irony can be seen to occur at this point in the historian's account. The reason for this is the operation of the pathetic fallacy. "Forces," trends, groups, institutions brought into tension with each other will tend to be apprehended anthropomorphically, under the analogy of human interactions. So no matter what the subjects might be of historical narrative, there will be a dramatic undertone to their interaction just because it

30

is narrative.

But when these same subjects and interactions are depersonified by a correlative appeal to nomothetic-deductive analysis for the sake of another kind of understanding, we have changed the point of view. Social agencies and natural forces which the narrative was covertly and inevitably humanizing are now treated as impersonal factors and scientific objects. It is not that the human has been restored to the context of natural processes but, rather, that the processes of all-inclusive nature must be dehumanized to be made amenable to mathematization or nomologization. The structural contrast, noticed or unnoticed, between the two perspectives is such that it is technically called ironic.

Narrative sentences can identify antecedents of given consequences, but they do not assert invariable antecedents or universally necessary consequents as such. "In came the military; out went social reform." But what about the officers who instituted a democratically oriented program of social reform in Peru? In what way did they "come in" and was the reform regressive or progressive in what respects? What such sentences assert or describe is the operation of human and other agencies in the realm of action. They deal in efficient causes, as Aristotle called them: the agencies by means of which what occurred was brought about. If agents are efficacious in bringing about particular events, why are not these agents "causes," and these events effects? Why can't a cause be asserted without asserting a causal law? This latter condition is required only by Hempel's formalism, not by any analysis of the terms cause and effect. By formalistic fiat Hempel's covering laws are required as a "guarantee" of any causal linkage asserted by single sentences, as if David Hume had not shown that there can be no such guarantee, and as if Hempel wanted to make the universe safe again by making all occurrences in it deductive.

Hempel's assumption about causality has the peculiar effect of denying that the causal relation can hold between terms that are unique or individual. As S. Lamprecht says (MN 1929, 1936; p. 81),

"Events are not causal because they occur according to certain uniformities and manifest certain invariant correlations which we can...discover and signi-

ficantly state...we properly call events causal because of the forceful activities of the particular
agents at work and in operation....the world is not
causal because it is ordered: rather it is causal
because particular agents are responsible for the
particular events within the texture of which, the
order is then found."

Now, the covering laws required by Hempel's model
of explanation are just this, one important kind of
pattern which functions as a "formal cause." The
patterns of expectation which narrative uses to present
a fictional or historical reality also function as part
of the formal cause of novels or histories. The formal
cause in works of literature is otherwise mainly made
up of the precedents in the genre technically and
creatively (formally) viewed: the ways in which stories
have been or can be told. In histories, the strict
general constraint upon the ways of narrative will be
the verifiability of the constitutive interconnections
suggested by the historian. But the uniformities,
whether under the constraint of the evidence or of the
imagination, are not the causes of the narrative,
except in the Aristotelian sense, any more than
Hempel's covering laws, as postulated uniformities, are
the causes of natural or historical events.

What Aristotle means by the formal cause of a work
can best be understood by relating it to the design of
a work. It is the architectonic according to which the
work was worked out or dianoetically shaped, the work
itself being a dynamic integration of the themes and
gestalts in it, vitally coordinated into a satisfactor-
ily coherent whole. So far as the design of a history
coincides with the presentational strategy or aesthetic
plan of its constructor, it will also overlap with the
"final cause" of a work, namely, with the relevant
practical or statesmanly reasons for the sake of which
the historian undertook his history. Even if initially
extra-aesthetic, these should be finally transformed
into pervasive qualities of the work. To the degree
that the formal cause can be internalized as a developed ability or knowledgeable responsiveness, to that
degree it is a part of the maker or efficient cause of
the history. And, to that degree, it overlaps with the
final causes of what he does as a historian.

The material cause of a narrative history, that
out of which it is made, is also complex. The materials
to which the history must give shape are as mixed as

32

the kinds of evidence that historians use, and as "non-material" or thematic as the storyteller's or social critic's are. There is no "raw" material that does not come with some thematic suggestions or contextual associations. In becoming part of the medium of the history these associations are exploited, counteracted or transformed in one way or another. So far as various materials come to the historian's hand with their own usable formalisms, the material cause of his work can be said to overlap with the formal cause. But all of the evidentiary material used by a historian does not get incorporated or reshaped into his history. Its value will then have been simply instrumental or ancillary.

It is in its aspect as something reflectively made or to be made, that history is both a practical science and a productive one. It is certainly not a theoretical science in the sense that either its procedures or its results can be systematically codified or deductively organized. History is a _praxis_ requiring and using an experience that cannot always be verbalized, and an accuracy that cannot always be quantified. What is verbalizable about this practice gets verbalized as "theory of history," and what can be quantified should be quantified if credibility is enhanced by denumeration. But history, like art and politics, is not pursued for the sake of theory in the deductivist sense.

Theories of human nature or theories of civilization which are sometimes extracted from histories, are necessarily speculative, extrapolative or partial. In such speculation, historical materials are being used as _dehistoricized_ evidence for or against a hypothesis in some other special science. The hypothesis is then reintroduced into the narrative world or cumulative advance of the history where, because it is a special-science hypothesis, it invites the making of predictions within the universe of discourse of the history itself. A pseudo-historical power of prophecy is thus attributed to a special-science hypothesis which that hypothesis does not have back in the abstracted world of dehistoricized biological, sociological or political events.

Back in this world of events the historian uses all kinds of working hypotheses in the process of constructing his history, but the history itself will be addressed to a _historical_ clarification of human doings and undergoings, that is _sui generis_ and inter-disciplinary. By historical is meant, in terms of the consequential order of a set of events in an ongoing process. In this way, history is a cognitive modality not only because it is propositional (assertive judgment) but because it is also a literary product (exhibitive judgment) and a practice of interrogating (active judgment) the very past which it is reconstructing from the evidence and which it is trying to understand and make available.

Bibliography

EDLE   1671. J. Locke _An_ _Early_ _Draft_ _of_ _Locke's_ _Essay_, ed. Aaron & Gibb (Oxford 1936)

PMPN   1686. I. Newton _Principia_ _Mathematica_ _Philosophiae_ _Naturalis_ (London: Royal Society); Florian-Motte trans. ed. Cajori (U. of Calif. Press 1962), 2 vols.

EHU   1690. J. Locke _An_ _Essay_ _concerning_ _Human_ _Understanding_ (London T. Basset); text ed. by P.H. Nidditch (Oxford 1979)

MA   1788. J.L. Lagrange _Mecanique_ _Analitique_; 2 ed.: _Mecanique_ _Analytique_ 2 vols. (Paris: Courcier 1811-1815)

PP   1813. J. Austen _Pride_ _and_ _Prejudice_: a Novel (London: T. Egerton 1813)

ZKNG   1824. L. von Ranke _Zur_ _Kritik_ _Neurer_ _Geschichtschreiber_, eine beylage zu desselben _Geschichte_ _der_ _Romanischen_ _und_ _Germanischen_ _Voelker_ (Leipzig & Berlin: Reimer 1824); tr. G.R. Dennis (London: Bell 1909). _The_ _Varieties_ _of_ _History_ ed. F. Stern (N.Y. Meridien 1956) pp. 54-63.

SPP   1824. A. Comte "Plan des Travaux necessaires pour reorganiser la Societe," publ. as _Systeme_ _de_ _Politique_ _Positive_ Vol. I, Part 1 Catechisme des industriels (Cahier 3) ed. C.H. de Saint-Simon (Paris 1824). Also in _Le_ _Producteur_ 1824. "Considerations philosophiques sur les Sciences et les Savants, _Le_ _Producteur_ No. 8 (1825)

LLJL   1829. P. King _The_ _Life_ _and_ _Letters_ _of_ _John_ _Locke_ with extracts from his Journals & Commonplace books (London 1829; repr. Bell 1864)

CPhP   1830-1842 A. Comte _Cours_ _de_ _Philosophie_ _Positive_ 6 vols. (Paris: Bachelier 1830-1842)

SPP   1851-1854 A. Comte _Systeme_ _de_ _Politique_ _Positive_ 4 vols. (Paris: Mathias)

CPS   1853. G.H. Lewes Comte's Philosophy of the Sci-
        ences (London: Bohn 1853)

SW   1873- L. von Ranke Saemmtliche Werke 54 vols.
        1890 (Leipzig: Duncker & Humblot); see The
              Theory and Practice of History ed. & tr.
              Iggers & Konrad (N.Y. Bobbs-Merrill 1973)
              for guidance.

MEHKD   1883. E. Mach Die Mechanik in ihrer Entwickelung
              historisch-kritisch dargestellt (Leipzig:
              Brockhaus); tr. Menger, ed. McCormack The
              Science of Mechanics (Open Court reprint)

CP   1902 C.S. Peirce "Coenoscopy," in review of
              E.C. Richardson's Classification, Theoret-
              ical and Practical. Repr. in Collected
              Papers I.241 (Harvard 1931)

CP   1903. C.S. Peirce "Coenoscopy," in notice of J.
              Fiske's Cosmic Philosophy. Repr. in Coll-
              ected Papers VI.6 (Harvard 1935)

CP   1905. C.S. Peirce "Coenoscopy," in rev. of Wundt
              Principles of Physiological Psychology.
              Repr. Coll. Papers VIII.199, 201 (Harvard
              1958)

EI   1905. E. Mach Erkenntnis und Irrtum (Leipzig:
              Barth 1905)

LR   1905- G. Santayana The Life of Reason: or The
        1906 Phases of Human Progress. I Reason in
              Common Sense, II Reason in Society, III
              Reason in Religion, IV Reason in Art, V
              Reason in Science (N.Y. Scribner's Sons)

PH   1916. F.J.E. Woodbridge The Purpose of History
              (N.Y. Columbia 1916)

PrH   1918. F.J. Teggart The Processes of History (New
              Haven: Yale 1918)

DW   1918- O. Spengler Der Untergang des Abendlaendes
        1922 2 vols. (Munich: Beck 1918-22; tr. C.F.
              Atkinson (N.Y. Knopf 1926-28): The Decline
              of the West

TH   1925. F.J. Teggart Theory of History (New Haven:
              Yale 1925)

MMM   1925. J.H. Randall _The Making of the Modern Mind_
           1 ed. 1926; 2 rev. ed. (Boston: Houghton
           Mifflin 1940)

RM   1926. F.J.E. Woodbridge _The Realm of Mind_ (N.Y.
           Columbia 1926)

MN   1929- S. Lamprecht _The Metaphysics of Naturalism_
           1967 (N.Y. Appleton). Essays from 1929-1966.

PLF   1941. K. Burke _The Philosophy of Literary Form_
           (Lousianna State U.P. 1941)

FGLH   1942. C. Hempel "The Function of General Laws in
           History," _The Journal of Philosophy_ Vol.
           39 (1942)

AEPS   1951. A. Einstein _Albert Einstein: Philosopher_
           Scientist ed. P.A. Schilpp (N.Y. Tudor
           1951)

TGT   1951. J. Buchler _Toward A General Theory of_
           Human Judgment (N.Y. Columbia 1951)

NJ   1955. J. Buchler _Nature and Judgment_ (N.Y. Col-
           umbia 1955)

NHE   1958. J.H. Randall _Nature and Historical Experi-_
           ence (N.Y. Columbia 1958)

CP   1962- J.H. Randall _The Career of Philosophy_ 3
           1977 vols. (N.Y. Columbia 1962-1977); vol. III
           ed. by B. Singer

SS   1961. E. Nagel _The Structure of Science_ (N.Y.
           Harcourt Brace 1961)

CM   1961. J. Buchler _The Concept of Method_ (N.Y.
           Columbia 1961)

HPUP   1963. J.H. Randall _How Philosophy Uses Its Past_
           (N.Y. Columbia 1963)

MSS   1964. A.J. Ayer _Man as a Subject for Science._
           Comte Memorial Lecture No. 6 (London:
           Athlone Press 1964)

AHI   1965. V. Tejera _Art and Human Intelligence_ (N.Y.
           Appleton-Century 1965)

FHK   1965. M. White <u>Foundations of Historical Knowl-edge</u> (N.Y. Harper 1965)

APH   1965. A. Danto <u>Analytical Philosophy of History</u> (Cambridge U.P. 1965)

MNC   1966 J. Buchler <u>Metaphysics of Natural Com-plexes</u> (N.Y. Columbia 1966)

NYRB   1967. A. Danto <u>The New York Review of Books</u> Feb. 23, 1967, p. 14

OKHP   1973. M. Murphey <u>Our Knowledge of the Historical Past</u> (N.Y. Bobbs-Merrill 1973)

CW   1978. J. Buchler "On the Concept of 'the World'," <u>The Review of Metaphysics</u> Summer 1978

PIN   1978. J. Buchler "Probing the Idea of Nature," <u>Process Studies</u> Vol. 8, No. 3 (1978)

Chapter III

A "Realist," a "Visionary," an "Experimentalist"
Woodbridge, Santayana, Mead

F.J.E. Woodbridge (1867-1940)

What makes historical accounts intelligible, Woodbridge says in The Purpose of History, is their selectivity about the past. By adding that history "is a kind
of human knowledge," Woodbridge means to say that histories conceptualize whatever they are the history of,
as having a "career" in time. Histories, in other
words, tend to biographize whatever they are the account of; they tend to see their subject as having a
life-cycle.

According to Woodbridge, this is what permits end-
events in a process to be seen as consequences of
preceding events. It allows the climactic behaviors of
groups or individuals to be seen as achievements or
goals. The historian's shaping of his account, and his
conception of what is relevant to it, is partly determined by the form of the type of life-cycle under the
analogy of which he sees his subject unfolding. The
analogy creates an acceptable form for the temporal
ordering of the relevant events.

Thus, the acceptability of the historian's ordering of events is partly due to the fact that the implicit analogy with the life-cycle is a first defense
against taking what is not human as a standard for what
is human, namely, human action and production. This
allows the historian to specify the material conditions
within which agents act, producers produce or events
occur, without reductively "materializing" the human
process--as happens in the scientistic or materialist
histories which try to be completely determinist. It is
evident that any history which sees man as (at least
partly) self-determining, will have a tendency to an-
thropomorphize material processes.

To ascribe patterns to nature is already, according to Woodbridge, to "speak figuratively" (PH p.
47f.). As importantly, it is to admit that "nature is
discovered to be an historical process, the conversion
of the possible into the actual in such a way
that...a...record of that conversion is conserved."
Researchers accustomed to seeing nature in terms of
non-temporal structures need to recover this insight,

39

upon which Dewey and Santayana also insisted (EN p. 163 and passim; AFSL p. 14f., RS p. 28ff.). Dewey's ironic plaint, in his great work of 1925, turns out to have been prophetic of the state of the question today: "The case of history is typical and basic. Upon the current view, it is a waste of time to discuss whether there can be such a thing as a science of history. History and science are by definition at opposite poles." Nelson Goodman's remark, made within another tradition (FFF 1955, p. 26), is apposite here, that the laws of nature are called laws because we use them to make predictions and not the other way around.

That a law is not used for prediction because it literally describes a causal connection, the thinkers who are my subject would agree. The pragmatists among them would add that, in practice, a natural law is a kind of directive for translation, via an operational hypothesis, into experimental operations. What has happened is that hypothetical connections which have been certified experimentally, are generalized into universasl form for purposes of deductive treatment. The universal is then misconceived as a timeless relation, and the false metaphysical problem arises of how a "timeless" pattern can apply to the temporal processes of nature. This misformulation also leads, conversely, to the spatialization of time and the reduction of temporal phenomena to non-temporal structures.

In connection with his discussion of "continuity" Woodbridge (PH p. 82) called "the laws of nature" the conditions "conformably to which whatever is done must be done." This coincides with the hypothetical sort of necessity that Aristotle ascribes to the order of earthly events. By "continuity" in the course of events Woodbridge meant that

> "nothing is so novel or distinct that it is wholly cut off from antecedents and consequents of some sort....every action of time, every conversion of the possible into the actual, is intimately woven into the order of events and finds there a definite place and definite connections."

The same hold for the course of human events:

> "More generally expressed the continuity of history is the continuity of matter. It comprises in sum the structure to which every moment in time is subject....But in itself [matter] is inert and impo-

tent. Activity of some sort must penetrate it, if
there is to be anything effected. And what is
effected reveals, when experimentally understood,
the laws as limitations within which the control of
any movement is possible." (PH p. 82)

These words at once call for two remarks by the
historical critic. It will remembered that, for Aristotle, matter as pure potentiality had to have been
always in motion (JHP 1973, p. 111f.). Secondly, the
cultural critic has to add that knowledge of the limiting conditions (in the sense of the material conditions) within which a deliberative product was a-
chieved, is sociohistorical knowledge. It would not
exhaust what remains to be articulated about the significance of the product as art or science or statesmanship. This significance demands to be understood in its
own terms or in terms true to its emergent and observable artistic, scientific or political design.

While Woodbridge emphasized the selective character of histories he was equally emphatic about the
"pluralistic" nature of history in the sense of the
human past. The main philosophic implication of this
pluralism for Woodbridge was that the complexity of
human history negates in advance all absolutist preten-
sions that particular histories might ever have (PH p.
52).

"For history is just the denial of absolute
considerations. It is the affirmation of relative
considerations, of considerations which are relative
to a selected career. There is no other kind of
history possible."

That histories are necessarily relative does not, of
course, entail that they are futile. But it does explain why there will always be many kinds of history,
as well as why philosophic historiography--unlike historians' historiography--may not be prescriptive and
must try to be pluralistic itself.

The most deepseated reasons, in my estimation, for
Woodbridge's insistence on the complexity of human
history were his characteristic repudiation of (i)
reductionism, of "clarity" purchased at the cost of
real complexity, and (ii) of the notion "that nature
has been framed in accordance with some preconceived
plan" (PH p. 48). The sharpness of his rejection can be
sensed in the memorable passage where he conjoins the

determinism of scientistic nomologism, if I may call it that, with the determinism of astrology (PH p. 53):

> "Those who seek to read their destiny from the cons-tellations ascendant at their birth are generally called superstitious; but those who seek to read it from the constitution of matter, or from the mechan-ism of the physical world, or from the composition of chemical substances, although no less supersti-tious, are too frequently called scientists."

George Santayana (1863-1952)

The two leading questions which Woodbridge built into his title The Purpose of History were (i) what are histories for, and (ii) is the human past pointed towards some great goal? This deliberately double-barrelled approach was not original to Woodbridge, however. Santayana had already found it appropriate in 1906, in his eloquent chapter on history in Reason in Science. What made the approach apposite was the composite nature of the target, namely, the combination of naive teleologism (about nature) with dogmatic moral fictions in accounts that purported to be histories or philosophies of the over-all course of human events.

Santayana no doubt had in mind such influential examples as Augustine's The City of God (c. 412 A.D.) or Bossuet's Discourse on Universal History (1681) or Fichte's The Vocation of Man (1800) or Hegel's The Philosophy of History (1822-1831) or Comte's account of "the general evolution of intelligence" at the beginning of his Course of Positive Philosophy (1830-1842). Santayana's response to the sheer arbitrariness of these kinds of history is still salutary (RS p.41):

"our progress of two centuries and our philosophies of history, embracing one-quarter of the earth for three thousand years, seem puerile vistas indeed. Shall all eternity and all existence be for the sake of what is happening here to-day, to me? Shall we strive manfully to the top of this particular wave, on the ground that its foam is the culmination of all things for ever?"

Only a humanist who was also, like Santayana, a naturalist could have such glimpses into the cosmic process, unfiltered through the humanizing spectacles of history, as the following (BROE p. 36),

"the true nerve, or rather the total dynamism, of events is not on the human scale; it is not picturesque; it is not to be divined dramatically or in moral terms. It is all the complex vegetative life of nature, the vast tangle of all derivations."

Santayana is usually classified as a materialist, but there is something definitely existentialist as well as visionary in his view of nature and contingency (AFSL p. 141):

43

"contingency of existence, no matter what you may believe to exist, always remains absolute, and the universe as a whole, having nothing before it or beside it, necessarily rejoices in the freedom of indifference, and is as it is without any cause....Even if, as a matter of fact, nothing were ever added to substance or changed in natural law...this very constancy would be a contingent fact, which conceivably might have been otherwise; so that determinism itself, if it rules the world, rules it by chance. The necessity or inertia which compels things to go on as they have hitherto is but a challengeable habit; and the fatality that first adopted this constitution for the universe may have adopted it...for a time only, to be exchanged, after so many revolutions...for a different rhythm."

Here, as historiographers, we must not fail to note that even when Santayana keeps the metaphors to a minimum, his discourse on the inhuman cannot help rehumanizing it in the expression of it. No matter that Santayana was not writing history here; it is the tendency of all human discourse to make its objects matter to us. History, in so far as it is narrative discourse and in so far as it is about the human past, will appear to be doing this more than other kinds of discourse. Santayana himself believed that all discourse is metaphoric or symbolic (OS p. 134ff.).

Where we would say that history is a human science, Santayana boldly asserted that "historical investigation is the natural science of the past" (RS p. 36). In qualification he added that it is a "natural science" that "labors under the disadvantage of not being able to appeal to experiment" just because it deals with the past. The facts of history are, therefore, hypothetical for him; they are inferred facts. And "a hypothetical fact is a...dangerous creature, since it lives on the credit of a theory which in turn would be bankrupt if the fact should fail." Santayana willingly concedes that hypotheses in history can be tested only against current events (RS p. 36f.); for, no other verification is available than that afforded by "present existence." Santayana is talking here of the investigative phases of history rather than about history writing as a whole. And familiarity with his style will help the reader to take his use of the term natural science in this passage as connoting "natural history," as it used to be called, rather than theoretical science.

Santayana does not deny that knowledge is one of the things that history offers. But about scientific knowledge itself, he records a significant proviso (RS p. 26):

"Understanding is nothing but seeing under and seeing far. There is indeed a great mystery in knowledge, but this mystery is present in the simplest memory or presumption. The sciences have nothing to supply more fundamental than vulgar thinking or...preliminary to it. They are...elaborations of it; they accept its presuppositions and carry on its ordinary processes. A pretence on the philosopher's part that he could get behind or below human thinking, that he could underpin...his own childhood and the...conventions of daily thought, would be pure imposture....Every deeper investigation presupposes ordinary perception and uses...its data. Every possible discovery _extends_ human knowledge. None can base human knowledge anew on a deeper foundation or prefix an ante-experimental episode to experience."

Here, as elsewhere in Santayana's work, it dawns upon his reader that the visionary quality of his thought is effectively "purified...by self-knowledge" (RS p. 42). So far can so enjoyably discursive a thinker be said to be also a Socratic.

Now theory, in the sense of "a schema of the relations among things" (RS p. 34) is, for Santayana as it was for Francis Bacon, "an expedient to cover ignorance and remedy confusion."

"The function of history, if it could be thoroughly fulfilled, would be to render theory unnecessary. Did we possess a record of all geological changes since the creation we should need no geological theory to suggest...what those changes must have been....The ideal historian, since he would know all the facts, would need no hypotheses...[or] classifications."

With this insight Santayana allows us to see that there is an inbuilt tendency in the enterprise of history which precludes its finished products from accepting the nomothetic-deductive form so dear to some epistemologists. Historians, like other explorers, must use working hypotheses to begin their searches, to organize or reorganize the evidence as it comes in, to help give shape to their presentations. But a working hypothesis is not a law of nature; its function is ancillary or, as Dewey would say, instrumental. And because the presentation of his work, the communication of his results, is inevitably also a matter of rhetoric or art, the historian cannot avoid being a humanist of some sort as well as a user of the special sciences. Clio was not Santayana's ruling Muse, any more than she is the Muse to epistemologists who write only for other epistemolgists. But, for all his skepticism, Santayana respected Clio enough to refrain, in his characterization of histories, from reducing her to either purely rhetorical tropes or to purely nomological schematizations.

We saw in the previous chapter that the predictions which histories make can be no better than those of the social sciences which they employ. Santayana identifies for us the fallacious mechanism in the rhetorical figure with which some historians appear to be making prophecies without formally appealing to any science (RS p. 40):

"We translate the necessity...lurking under life's commonplace yet unaccountable shocks, into verbal principles, names for general...results that play some role in our...philosophy. Each of these idols of the theatre is visible on only a single stage and to...predisposed spectators....Such a manipulation of history...ends in asserting that events have directed themselves prophetically upon the interests which they arouse."

Now it is partly under "theory" that interpretation fits, for Santayana, in his handy division of the pursuit of history into three overlapping parts: "investigation, theory, and story-telling." And the function of theory, as we saw, is to fill the gaps in our inductive knowledge. So "historical theory, in turn, is a falsification of causes, since no causes are other than mechanical;...[historical theory] dissolves in the presence either of adequate knowledge or clear ideals."

As such causes are "for scientific inference to discover" (RS p. 42). Santayana's last word on "causes" in history had better be given here:

"the aim pursued and attained is not the force that operates, since the result achieved had many other conditions besides the worker's intent, and that intent itself had causes which it knew nothing of. Every 'historical force' pompously appealed to breaks up on inspection into a cataract of miscellaneous natural processes and minute particular causes. It breaks into its mechanical constituents and proves to have been nothing but an _effet d'ensemble_ produced on a mind whose habits are essentially rhetorical" (RS p.42f.).

[A concrete confirmation of Santayana's point can be found in the economic historian who said "no law of nature compels a free market economy to suffer from recessions or periodic inflations." The statement also implies that so-called economic "forces" are not underlying conditions in the natural-science sense, but the runaway results of human actions and insufficient social policy and science (_Economic Report of the President_, U.S.A. 1965). It is noteworthy that recent epistemological philosophy of history nowhere gives credit to Santayana for his analytic distinction, in connection with human action, between the "causes of" and "the reasons for" an action. To give philosophic credit where it is due would, presumably, be to "do history," where all an epistemologist is required to "do" is "philosophy."]

Next, when interpretations of the human past are part of "story-telling," they "become...legitimate" (RS p. 42) to the extent that they make explicit to the reader the ideals which are governing the interpreter's claims. Interpretation, honestly self-defined as "imagination and will," legitimately becomes "a sort of retrospective politics, an estimate of events in reference to the moral ideal" which "might supervene upon history."

In a self-reference to _The Life of Reason_, Santayana adds that such an estimate can well be called a philosophy of history because it is a reflective operation performed on scientific investigations undertaken to provide a basis for, and illustration of, the ideal. Now, both because histories can always be revised and because the moral imagination can--in romance, epic and tragedy--disengage itself from all allegiance to particular facts, Santayana is convinced that history "is a provisional discipline." The philosophic reader is led to ask, does Santayana therefore think that philosophies of history are also provisional exercises?

The historian of historiography does not need
Santayana to see that those philosophies of history
which mainly reflect a dominant dogma or an intellectual fashion or a partial if plausible formulation of
the problems of history, are certifiably provisional.
The clarification obtainable from Santayana follows
from his pluralism, his generous sense of values and an
equation of the philosopher of history with the historian (RS p.43):

"the historian, in estimating what has been hitherto
achieved, needs to make himself the spokesman for
all past aspirations."

Reciprocally, the equation seems to require the historian to become if not a philosopher, at least an intellectual historian of human "aspirations." This does not
make Santayana's philosophic historiography "prescriptive." It is rather the unargued result of the observation that there are no social histories that are not
also histories of belief, and that good social histories have always deliberately used, or been, intellectual histories in the sense of histories of belief.

Since, for Santayana, all standards or ideals
against which interpretations are judged are themselves
arbitrary, offshoots of their time and place, he is
obliged to spell out how he thinks a critique or interpretation of the past may be judged to be more or less
just. In the review of a historical interpretation,
only an "enlightened" standard or ideal would be a
"touchstone for estimation." To be enlightened an ideal
has to recognize that its own legitimacy is conditioned. As a <u>historical</u> touchstone it would be cogni-
zant of the validity of other ideals relative to other
conditions (RS p. 43).

Whenever individuals or nations become reflective
they give expression to their ideals and aspirations. A
historical judge "who does not wish to be...irrational"
will have made the sympathetic study of these
aspirations a precondition of his appraisal. He will be
practiced in assuming a variety of points of view and
in "considering all real interests affected."

If, like Santayana, he is interested in the history of human rationality, he should not claim to know
ahead of time what the highest form of rationality is
or "what ultimate form the good might some day take"
(RS p. 43). He will avoid what I call "the arrogance of

48

philosophism;" he will not "make the purposes of the philosopher himself,...the test of all excellence." On the contrary, "impartial historical investigation" and the reconstruction of the moral life of the past will help him to clarify and redefine his own ideals.

It is the historian's interest in the good and the human that makes the discipline of history multiple in its functions, and that makes the historian "a politician and a poet" as well as "a man of science." It is this interest that can make the history of part of the past appear to have a moral. The scientific scruples of the circumstantial historian notwithstanding, "certain men and certain episodes will retain...their intrinsic nobility." Naturally, "what makes the story worth telling is its pertinence to the political and emotional life of the present." And, practiced in this context, history acquires "the function of epic or dramatic poetry" (RS p. 45). Another context, and other, more sordid or pedestrian interests can turn the account of a past into a kind of technological or psychological "gossip" or "petty historical drama" (RS p. 46). Tragic histories, epic histories have to engage objectively the deepest concerns and greatest interests of a people if they are to function as epics or Tragedies in the life of that people.

These events--as Thucydides was the first to point out and as Santayana reminds us (RS p. 47)--have to have achieved the level of the mythical (HPW I, 21). "The principle that elicits histories out of records," says Santayana, "is the same that breeds legends out of remembered events" (RS p. 32f.). "The successful historical poet," he adds (RS p. 47), "would be he who caught the most significant attitude which a person in [a fateful] position could possibly have assumed, and his [character]...would be essentially a mythical person." As for the plots in which historical heroes are embedded, Santayana is again insightful, "what is interesting is brought forward as if it had been central and efficacious in the march of events, and harmonies are turned into causes" (RS p. 33). A function of history, then, "is to lend materials to politics and to poetry" (RS p. 48).

Finally,

"A good book of history is one that helps the statesman to formulate and to carry out his plans, or that helps the tragic poet to conceive what is most glorious in human destiny."

Santayana's concentration on the several functions of history did not keep him from observing their epistemological context. To begin with "sense is the foundation of everything" (RS p. 49).

"Yet memory rather than sense is knowledge in the pregnant acceptation...; for in sense object and process are hardly distinguished whereas in memory...the present vouches for the absent. Similarly history...is superior to [memory]; for while it ...extends memory...it shows a higher logical development than memory has and is riper for ideal uses....[Historical] information is not...idle knowledge; it truly _informs_ or shapes the mind, giving it new aptitudes."

Just as "conscience needs to be controlled by experience if it is to become rational," so "civic man" needs to know the past in order to be actively true to the good in it. "[A] memory of what human experience has been, a sense of what it is likely to be under specific circumstances gives the will a new basis." This makes of history both a precondition of human dignity and a help in the pursuit of a happiness which is not merely personal.*

* A report on Santayana's conception of history would be remiss if it did not draw attention to the extraordinary and accurate anticipation, in Chapter II of _Reason in Science_, of the epoch-making work, twenty years later, of the Homeric scholar Milman Parry (ETH 1928, FMH 1928; MHV). Parry's demonstration of the oral-aural nature of the compositional process in preliterate epic verse-making both fleshes out, and finds its rationale in Santayana's prescient paragraphs (RS p. 31-32).

George Herbert Mead (1863-1931)

More than any other thinker Santayana helps us to see that "American Naturalism" and "Anglo-French Positivism" are both of them faiths. The first is an imaginative faith, steeped in the humanities and social sciences, that does not over-interpret the natural sciences. The second is a faith in an interpretation of science that has nothing positive to say about the humanities.--John Stuart Mill's tribute, in his Autobiography (1873), to the spiritual efficacy of poetry is the original exception. [The Early Draft of John Stuart Mill's Autobiography edited by J. Stillinger should also be consulted. This draft dates back to c. 1854.]

While all the "American naturalists" considered here have understood the importance of science to the human process, it is Mead more than his peers who stands out as primarily interested in the scientific enterprise and its assumptions. Committed as he was to the methodology of the sciences, Mead could not accept as scientific the finality of Minkowski's assumption that the true order of things is transcendentally fixed in a four-dimensional space-time continuum in which time is assimilated to a spatial dimension resulting in an eternal now (PP 1932). He saw that Minkowski's assumption, which Whitehead felt confirmed his own views (CN 1920), was a metaphysical move and not part of relativity physics. And it implied that change and time are not true characteristics of the world of events but only subjective interpretations of it.

So, Mead says in The Philosophy of the Present:

"It is the task of the philosophy of today to bring into congruence with each other [the] universality of determination which is the text of modern science, and the emergence of the novel which belongs not only to the experience of human social organisms, but is found also in a nature which science and the philosophy that has followed it have separated from human nature" (p. 14).

As conveyed by this passage Mead's philosophic project was at least twofold. Philosophy must recategorize nature in a way such that a human nature which is social can be reincorporated in it, and made continuous with it. Philosophy must also reconcile the cognitive determinism of the sciences with the facts of change, both in an eventful world and in the self-determining individual (PA p. 108f.; Mead's own word is "self-conditioning").

Mead's success in this endeavor was predicated on his development of an adequate theory of time. It is therefore not surprising, in retrospect, that Mead's theory of time is not only the middle term between the natural sciences and the human sciences, but is also the basis of the deepseated continuity between his philosophy of history and his philosophy of science. In respect to the unity of Mead's philosophy of history with his theory of time, we can also see that it presents a parallel with, perhaps a model for, the oneness of the theory of time and the theory of history in Woodbridge.

There is another important respect in which the latter is like Mead. Woodbridge perceived that the picture of nature which sees it as an unheeding congeries of relentless processes without appeal, is a falsification of nature because it leaves out mankind (AEN 1940, p. 149). The positive point retrievable from the picture, for Woodbridge, was its dramatization of an aspect of time, namely, its irreversible order or connectedness.

But this irreversibility is characteristic only of time, not of the past. For, one of the tenets which most distinguishes this generation of American philosophers and the next is, notoriously, the common insistence on the necessary revisability and hypothetical nature of the past. "Real" or experienced time, efficacious or productive time is always present time, as opposed to lapsed or future time which are recovered or posited in thought as abstractions.

Just as in Aristotle change is the substrate of time, so for Mead, time is a function of change (PP p. 28-31; PA p. 638). It is duration, not time, that is a function of consciousness. For Mead "[the] reality [of a past] is in its interpretation of the present" (PA p. 616). "What we have," Mead says, "is a passing present, compounded of the past which is determined by the interpretation of the present and the future which comes to us as alternative possibilities" (ibid.).

Mead's view that new pasts continuously emerge, and that there is no part of the now accepted past which is irrevocable, rests on assumptions derived from his observation of the process of research science and, no doubt, from his own pursuit of scientific knowledge. Mead saw that the function of research is not merely to gather information or even, as the epistemologists were beginning to claim, to "explain" phenomena nomologically (i.e. by subsuming them under appropriate "laws"). He saw science not as referring new phenomena to old laws, but as working to devise and test new hypotheses that would "account for" problematic data and anomalous phenomena in the sense of allowing some blocked advance or inhibited action to resume. New or problematic data become intelligible or manageable, not by resorting to old ways of interpreting or doing things but by means of a reconceived past or a newly constructed history. Thus, a past is as hypothetical as any future; and the validity of hypotheses about the past can only be tested in the present or by future experience: "the past is a working hypothesis that has validity in the present within which it works but has no other validity" (PA p. 96).

Mead is not lapsing, here, into the rigidities or anachronisms of "presentism" since, for him, what "the significant content which historical research reveals" is not "the past object as implied in the present." It is rather "a newly discovered present which can only be known and interpreted in the past which it involves (PA p. 94). This newly discovered present includes a "pictured extension which each generation...spread[s] behind itself [as its past]. One past displaces and abrogates another as inexorably as the rising generation buries the old" (PA p. 95).

The effective past is that which allows us to understand or "interpret" the present. "No scientist secure in his experimental method would base that security upon the agreement of its results with the structure of any changeless past...within his ken" (PA p. 96). Mead speaks of the present as something that is "interpreted" because our knowledge of it, too, is hypothetical. The question of the validity of a [hypothetical] past only arises in the presence of some problem. The verification of the hypothetical solution to the problem constitutes the solution as knowledge. For, that is knowledge, according to Mead, which solves problems (PA p. 95). And, as knowledge it "fits into the world that is there, so that we act with reference to it as we do with reference to the world that is there."

Furthermore, "so far as experience is concerned [it] is there also, until in conduct we find that it is not there; and then we have a problem on our hands and have to find out what is there--a problem of inference, of implication, of knowledge." And just as it is (our understanding of) the present that tests the past, so it is the future that will test the present which we are (hypothetically) defining to ourselves. To recapitulate: the past interprets the present, it does not fully determine it, though it is the present that makes the past selectively determinate. The sense in which "the past...is in the present" is that in which "the past is there conditioning the present and its passage into the future."

The future is chosen by the present as alternatives are realized among potentialities; but the actual future will test and reconstruct the present. The future, we can be sure, will not see us as we see ourselves.

It follows that those who know no history or have no sense of it, simply live in an impoverished and barely intelligible present. The reality of the historical past is, thus, not ontologically secondary. It is indispensable "to our present undertaking of interpreting our world...for [the sake of] present conduct and estimation" (PA p. 97). We can now recognize frankly "that the only reason for research into the past is the present problem of understanding a problematic world, and the only test of the truth of what we have discovered is our ability to so state the past that we can continue the conduct whose inhibition has set the problem to us."

Thus the function of the philosophy of history is not to predict the future, for it is not predictable in the sense required by the nomological view of historical studies. The latter view is true to its formalist understanding of the deductive sciences, but it is demonstrably not true to either the nature of the human past or the nature of historical query and the ways in which it presents its results. It is not scientific to assimilate new problems to pre-structured types of solution if the problems are really novel. It emerges that the deep contrary-to-fact implication of the nomological philosophy of history is its unstated inference that change in human affairs can be assumed to be always orderly, as it would have to be to be systematically explainable in a nomothetic-deductive way.

Because at present we do know that values will always change with time, Mead says, and because we know what sort of conditions favor or explain eventful changes we, in fact, do have "a philosophy of history" in the traditional sense. And this philosophy of history is different from the other-worldly philosophy of history of the West before the Renaissance (PA p. 503). In "the philosophy of history of church doctrine...all values were authoritatively defined and fixed." But as a matter of fact, for Mead,

"A philosophy of history arose as soon as men conceived that society was moving toward the realization of triumphant ends in some great far-off event" (PA p. 504).

The historical fact, unfortunately, has been that

"The histories that have most fastened upon men's minds have been political and cultural propaganda, and every great social movement has flashed back its light to discover a new past" (PA p. 94).

It would follow, for Mead and his reader, that the present cannot be coped with in a problem-solving way if the histories available to it are not scientifically sound, whatever the way in which they may be presented. This is why historical query must include a scientific dimension, and why philosophy of history must recognize that, variegated as the tasks of history are, the severest test of the adequacy of written histories is their contribution to an intelligent coping with present problems. Trenchant "factual" monographs and eloquent popular histories which affect the sensibilities of an epoch will only complicate its predicament if they lead into misinterpretations of the present. It will therefore be the task of the philosophy of history to uncover such slippages wherever and however they occur in the construction of histories and in the uses that are made of them. This insight is fundamental to Mead's conception of the philosophy of history:

"it is just this reinterpretation of values in the face of the problems of society that constitutes the subject matter of the philosophy of history, and it is the theory of this reinterpretation that is that philosophy" (PA p. 511).

In his observation of the methods of historical

research, Mead found two ideas about the past to be operating. There is a kind of plastic past with which we interrogate the problematic domain we have entered as historians. This past is working "when we are at grips with a problem and are seeking its solution....it takes on now one sense and now another; we are seeking its meaning, endeavoring to find in it the course we should follow" (PA p. 507). Then, once we have been able to formulate a solution to the problem "the whole falls into a single story that we read in terms of a [hypothetical] causal series....we build up a hypothesis which we test and perhaps act successfully upon, and then the problem takes the interpretation which our hypothesis places upon it." The outcome is a reconstruction of the meaning of the past for what we confront at present. Hypothetical as it is, this meaning is "always subject to conceivable reformulations, on the discovery of later evidence," as Mead had said in The Philosophy of the Present(p. 29).

The past is also conceived by Mead as the meaning of what happened in a present. So, if the analysis of meaning is the peculiarly philosophic activity that it is thought to be today, it follows that historical investigation is necessarily a philosophic activity in one of its phases. In this sense, historical studies that wish to be as fully reflective as possible cannot do without philosophy of history. On the other hand, philosophic analysis that wishes to be fully informed about the meanings it is analyzing, cannot ignore the social histories which have conditioned those meanings.

Mead's Wider Notion of "Experience"

Now, for Mead, experience is wider than consciousness. "The non-reflective act comes first," and "consciousness emerges upon the occasion of the reflective act," when there is a problem which arouses it. But "intelligence," which consists in the "appropriateness of the response of a living form to the environment," is not just "a character of mind" (PA p. 404). Mead insists "we confine the term 'intelligence' to the modification of the response and the selection of the stimulus as the result of past experience, in meeting difficulties that arise in the life-process." So, intelligence is not merely mental either: "as there is evidence of this adjustment in unicellular forms, and plants, and as it is found through ranges of our own conduct that are not usually considered mental, it is hardly appropriate to consider intelligence as such mental" (PA p. 404).

Thus, for Mead, non-reflective experience can be adjustive, even though for him experience as such is not problematic. It is simply the process within which problems arise. Occurring with the present, experience has no reference to either the past or the future. But it is not mere endurance since it is "conduct...regarded from the standpoint of the [living] form rather than...the environment....'experience' implies that one is giving a life-history of the form in question" (PA p. 405).

Since "experience" implies that the characters of things and events are stated in terms of their values for the individual as revealed in his conduct (whether conscious or not), we begin to see that experience for Mead is the implicated interactive basic process of the individual, as individual, assimilating and adjusting to the circumstantial present in which he lives. In retrospect, Mead's characterization of experience appears as a convincing anticipation of Buchler's notion of proception, and as a great improvement upon the unexamined notion of experience to be found in the epistemological tradition that restricts it to sensation, perception and conscious memory.

Bibliography

HPW   Thucydides <u>History</u> <u>of</u> <u>the</u> <u>Peloponnesian</u> <u>War</u>, 4
        vols. ed. & tr. C.F. Smith (Loeb
        Libr. 1919-23)

CG   c.412   A.D. Augustine <u>The</u> <u>City</u> <u>of</u> <u>God</u> 7 vols. ed.
                & tr. G.E. McCracken (Loeb 1957-72)

DHU   1681   J.B. Bossuet <u>Discours</u> <u>sur</u> <u>l'histoire</u>
                <u>universelle</u>, ed. augm. L.S. Auger (Paris:
                Lefevre 1825); tr. Forster (U. Chicago
                1976)

NS   1725   G.B. Vico <u>The</u> <u>New</u> <u>Science</u>; tr. of 3 ed. of
                1744 T. Bergin & M. Fisch (Cornell 1948)

VBG   1794   J.G. Fichte <u>Einige</u> <u>Vorlesungen</u> <u>ueber</u> <u>die</u>
                <u>Bestimmung</u> <u>des</u> <u>Gelehrten</u> (Jena: Gabler)

GGWL   1794   J.G.Fichte <u>Grundlage</u> <u>der</u> <u>Gesammten</u> <u>Wissen-</u>
                <u>schaftslehre</u> (Leipzig: Gabler 2 ed. 1801)

HVPHM   1796   N.C. de Condorcet <u>Outlines</u> <u>of</u> <u>an</u> <u>Historic-</u>
                <u>al</u> <u>View</u> <u>of</u> <u>the</u> <u>Progress</u> <u>of</u> <u>the</u> <u>Human</u> <u>Mind</u>,
                tr. from the French (Philadelphia: Lang &
                Ustick 1796)

BM   1800   J.G. Fichte <u>Die</u> <u>Bestimmung</u> <u>des</u> <u>Menschen</u>
                (Berlin: Voss)

GGZ   1806   J.G. Fichte <u>Die</u> <u>Grundzuege</u> <u>des</u> <u>Gegenwartig</u>
                <u>en</u> <u>Zeitalters</u>. Vorlesungen gehalten
                im Jahre 1804-5 (Berlin: Realschulbuch-
                handlung)

RDN   1808   J.G. Fichte <u>Reden</u> <u>an</u> <u>die</u> <u>Deutsche</u> <u>Na-</u>
                <u>tion</u> (Berlin: Realschulbuchhandlung)

VPG   1822-   G.W.F. <u>Hegel</u> <u>Vorlesungen</u> <u>ueber</u> <u>die</u> <u>Philo-</u>
        1831   <u>sophie</u> <u>der</u> <u>Geschichte</u>. The Philosophy of
                History, tr. J. Sibree; Prefaces by K.
                Hegel & C.J. Friedrich (N.Y. Dover repr.
                1956)

CPP   1830-   A. Comte <u>Cours</u> <u>de</u> <u>Philosophie</u> <u>Positive</u> 6
        1842   vols. 1842 (Paris: Bachelier 1830-42)

EPP   1844   K. Marx <u>Economic</u> <u>and</u> <u>Philosophic</u> <u>Manu-</u>
                <u>scripts</u> <u>of</u> <u>1844</u> (London: Lawrence & Wise-

hart 1959)

CHPR 1844   K. Marx _Critique of Hegel's Philosophy of Right_, tr. Jolin & O'Malley, Intro. & Notes (Cambridge U.P. 1970)

MP 1847   K. Marx _Misere de la Philosophie_ (Paris: A. Frank 1847)

FP 1857   H. Spencer "Progress; Its Laws and Cause," Westminster Review 1857. "The Ultimate Laws of Physiology," National Review 1857. Both incorporated in _First Principles_ 1862.

DK 1857   K. Marx General Introduction of _Das Kapital_ (ch. I-IX); Vol. I not publ. till 1867. _Capital_ 2 vols. tr. from 3 ed. Moore & Aveling; ed. F. Engels (London: Sonnenschein 1887)

CCPE 1858   K. Marx _Contributions to the Critique of Political Economy_ (Grundrisse der Kritik der Politischen Oekonomie), Intro. of 1859. Ed. & tr. I.N. Stone (London: K. Paul 1904)

OSNS 1859   C. Darwin _On the Origin of Species by Means of Natural Selection_ (London: J. Murray 1859)

FP 1862   H. Spencer _First Principles_ (N.Y. Rand McNally, repr. 1880)

AJS 1872   J.S. Mill _Autobiography_ ed. Helen Taylor (London: Longmans 1873). _The Early Draft of J.S. Mill's Autobiography_ ed. J. Stillinger (Urbana: U. of Illinois 1961), dated to c. 1854.

PCH 1874   F.H. Bradley _The Presuppositions of Critical History_ (Oxford: Parker 1874)

PS 1876-   H. Spencer _Principles of Sociology_ 3 vols.
    1896   (London: Williams & Norgate 1876-96)

EE 1893-   T.H. Huxley _Prolegomena to Evolution and Ethics_, and _Evolution and Ethics_ ed.
    1894   Julian Huxley (London: Pilot Press 1947)

CSRCA 1896   B. Croce _Il Concetto della Storia nelle sue Relazioni col Concetto dell'Arte_ (Roma: Loescher 1896); repr. w. two articles from the _Atti dell'Accademia Pontaniana_.

MSEM 1900   B. Croce _Materialismo Storico ed Economia Marxistica_ (Milano: Sandron 1900)

LR   1904-   G. Santayana _The Life of Reason_ 5 vols.
      1906   (N.Y. Scribner's): I Reason in Common Sense, II Reason in Society, III Reason in Religion, IV Reason in Art, V Reason in Science.

FGV   1911   B. Croce _La Filosofia di Giambattista Vico_ (Bari: Laterza)

NH   1912   J.H. Robinson _The New History_ (N.Y. Macmillan; repr. in 1965)

SSH   1913   B. Croce _Saggio sullo Hegel_ (Bari Laterza)

TPH   1915   B. Croce _Zur Theorie und Geschichte der Historigraphie_, aus dem italienischen uebersetzt von E. Pizzo (Tuebingen: Mohr 1915). _On History_, tr. D. Ainslie from the 2nd Italian ed. of 1919. Reprinted as _Theory and Practice of History_ (Russell & Russell)

PH   1916   F.J.E. Woodbridge _The Purpose of History_ (N.Y. Columbia)

LSK   1918   G. Santayana "Literal and Symbolic Knowledge," _Journ. of Philosophy_ 1918; repr. in _Obiter Scripta_ ed. Buchler & Schwartz (N.Y. Scribner's 1936)

DW   1918-   O. Spengler _Der Untergang des Abendlaendes_
      1922   2 vols. (Munich: Beck); tr. C.F. Atkinson _The Decline of the West_ (Knopf 1926-28)

NHSS 1925   H.E. Barnes _The New History and the Social Sciences_ (N.Y. Century)

EN   1925   J. Dewey _Experience and Nature_ (Chicago: Open Court; 2 ed. 1929)

MHV   1928   M. Parry _L'Epithete traditionelle dans Homere_: Essai sur un probleme de style homerique; and _Les Formules et la Metrique d'Homere_; now in _The Making of Homeric Verse_. Collected Papers of Milman Parry, ed. A. Parry (Oxford 1971)

EHJD 1929 G.H. Mead "The Nature of the Past," _Essays in Honor of John Dewey_ (N.Y. Holt 1929)

PP 1932 G.H. Mead _The Philosophy of the Present_ (La Salle: Open Court)

PE 1932 E. Cassirer _Die Philosophie der Aufklaerung_ (Tuebingen: Mohr); tr. Koelln & Pettegrove _The Philosophy of the Enlightenment_ (Princeton U.P. 1951)

MTNC 1936 G.H. Mead _Movements of Thought in the Nineteenth Century_ (U. of Chicago)

NH25 1936 C. Brinton "The New History: Twenty-Five Years After," _Journ. of Social Philosophy_ Vol. I (1936)

HATA 1938 B. Croce _La Storia come Pensiero e come Azione_ 2 ed. (Bari: Laterza); tr. as _History as the Story of Liberty_ (London: Allen & Unwin 1941)

PA 1938 G.H. Mead "History and the Experimental Method," and "Experimentalism as a Philosophy of History," in _The Philosophy of the Act_ ed. C. Morris (U. of Chicago 1938)

EON 1940 F.J.E. Woodbridge _An Essay on Nature_ (N.Y. Columbia 1940)

PLF 1941 K. Burke _The Philosophy of Literary Form_ (Louisiana State U.P.)

FGLH 1942 C. Hempel "The Function of General Laws in History," _The Journ. of Philos._, 39 (1942)

SP 1943 C. Wright Mills _Sociology and Pragmatism_ (U. of Wisconsin 1943; N.Y. Oxford 1964)

TPHS 1946 J.H. Randall and G. Haines "Controlling Assumptions in the Practice of American Historians," _Theory and Practice in Historical Study_ (N.Y. Soc.Sci.Research Council Bulletin No. 54, 1946)

FFF 1955 N. Goodman _Fact, Fiction and Forecast_ (Harvard 1955)

ERP 1965 G.P.O. _Economic Report of the President_ (Washington: Govt. Printing Office 1965)

BROE 1967 G. Santayana "On Idealistic Historians," _The Birth of Reason and Other Essays_ ed. D. Corey (N.Y. Columbia 1967)

AFSL 1967 G. Santayana "Inevitable Contingency of All Fact," _Animal Faith and Spiritual Life_ ed. J. Lachs (N.Y. Appleton-Century)

RTCE 1971 V. Tejera Review of _Tempo, Coscienza e Essere nella filosofia di Aristotele_ by L. Ruggiu, J. of the Hist. of Philos. XI, 1.

Chapter IV

Philosophic Practioners of History
H. Schneider and J.H. Randall

Schneider on the Succession of Philosophies

In his A History of American Philosophy Herbert
Schneider (b. 1892) differed implicitly and in practice
from Woodbridge's bold assertion that, as a study of
the generic traits of existence, metaphysics uses much
the same methods as the sciences. An explicit qualification of Woodbridge's claim can be found in an article
of c. 1972, "Why Philosophy Will Never Be a Science"
(repr. in PACA 1974). By "science" Schneider meant "the
cooperative and systematic search for experimental
evidence" (PACA p. 467). By "a philosophy" he meant
something which "as a whole must be characterized by
other predicates, not by true and false." [In the
reprinted sentence from which I have quoted, there has
to be a typographical error. The sense requires "any"
or "a" rather than "no"; but I have not been able to
verify this with the editors.]

When we realize that Woodbridge was using the term
science in its Aristotelian sense of effective knowledge and that Schneider is not denying that a philosophy can provide knowledge, the difficulty disappears.
But it is also clear that, to Schneider, the personal
element in a philosophy is not excisable from it: "Like
poetry and the other arts, philosophy is a personal
creation and expression, even in its aim at universality" (PACA p. 470). Furthermore: "The history of philosophy is not really cumulative as is the history of
science." And there is no philosophy which does not
either provide or imply "criteria for evaluation" or "a
sense of values" (ib. 471).

In the case of what is usually called science, its
nationality, its temporal and cultural circumstances
are accidental to it. In a philosophy, however, such
conditions are necessary to the understanding of it.
"Without literary embodiment...a philosophy is practic-
ally powerless. Philosophical writing....may be clumsy
as literature and dull as entertainment, but....the
idioms, nuances, and limitations of vernaculars are
much more serious for philosophical understanding than
they are for scientific research" (p. 472). More deeply, it is a philosophy's communicating of its sense of
what is important that seems to determine its readabil-

63

ity or viability for an audience. As an observant historian Schneider knows that, nonetheless, "philosophers have usually imagined themselves to be scientists and have represented themselves as seekers and finders of...objective truths" (p. 467).

The historical observer can only say that philosophers who continue to represent themselves in this way have failed to perceive that the succession of philosophic schools and styles which preceded, or have fed into, their own systems--were once as fashionable or credible as they believe themselves to be. It is as if such philosophers had not noticed that "each [of his predecessors also] conceive[d] of his ideas as the logical outcome of all previous thought" (p. 470). "Philosophers," says Schneider echoing one of Nietzsche's creative complaints, "make poor historians."

It is one of the strengths of the now neglected school of classic American philosophers that they had such a respect for history and put their knowledge of it to such good uses. The impact which a knowledge of the sociohistorical context of a philosophy or succession of philosophies has upon our understanding of that philosophy or that succesion, is so great as to be empirically undeniable. It can only be denied by fiat or by evasive or silent practices. But any practice of philosophy which neglects this aspect of itself makes unnecessary difficulties for itself and its readers. It also gives rise to systematically misleading conceptualizations. [This is concretely and abundantly illustrated in my "Intellectual History as a Tool of Philosophy," Papers of the Long Island Philosophy Society, Spring 1981, to be published in Against Anti-History in Philosophy ed. T. Lavine and V. Tejera (Nijhoff)].

The Historical Way and the Concept of "Career"

Now Schneider, who took his doctorate under the direction of John Dewey, could be counted as part of "the Woodbridge tradition" if the latter is defined as S. Lamprecht defined it, namely, "a sensitive manner of viewing the varied forms of human life and experience as conditioned by their context within the pattern of natural events" (NH 1950, p. vi). But there is another point on which Schneider differs from Woodbridge, and that is the assumption "that since persons have careers, their history must also be a career" (WB 1962, p. 55). Schneider rejected the analogical application of this notion to what he called "historical being."

64

But, judging from his practice in A History of American Philosophy, Schneider meant by "historical being" the human past itself rather than historical subjects or subject-matters. We can agree that it is futile to conceptualize the whole human past as a single career. It is too complex a process, with too many kinds of historical prevalence and too many kinds of determining factors and self-determining agents in it, to be narratable as a single story--as the career of mankind. But in his own account of N. American philosophy Schneider takes both single individuals and differentiable "traditions" of thought as the subjects of his history. So it is not the producers and products which together constitute culture that are not suscept-ible of narrative treatment on the pattern of a career; it is rather "cultural being," or human culture as a whole that cannot be treated as a career.

Consistently with his practice in A History of American Philosophy, Schneider's theoretical reflec-tions in Ways of Being allow us to see more expressly that he disapproved of, and avoided, giving accounts of thinkers and traditions in terms of their "rise and fall." Presumably, this was because of the tendentious nature of such terms. They tend to confuse accounts of the worldly emergence or success of a philosophy with accounts of its validity as a form of thought, as a method, as a serviceable or expressive construction.

However, we should not over-state Schneider's point and its implications. He does speak of a philoso-phy as having a "life-span" (PACA p. 471), thus appear-ing to acquiesce in Woodbridge's--and Randall's (CP 1962, p. x-xi)--model for treating historical subject-matters. [Randall, in the end, agrees with Schneider that there is a difference between "a history" and "a career." What he also believed was that modern philoso-phy was unified enough so that it could be said to have had a career. See below.]

Schneider's use of the term "life-span" corres-ponds to his stragegy of not depersonalizing the philo-sophies under study, or diminishing their philosophic vitality a priori by reducing them to abstractional units in a bodiless history of mere ideas (PACA p. 470). Schneider's practice avoids the explicit dramati-zation of his subjects' thought-systems while, nonethe-less, treasuring and recapturing "the philosophical life" in them.--In recognizing this about Schneider's

65

history we have not forgotten that no discourse can entirely avoid implicit dramatization of its subject, for the reason that discourse can use only human terms.-- Schneider was also making the point that part- icular philosophies have their existence and meaning in definable "cultural fields of operation" which it is the responsibility of the historian to delineate and specify. "The life-span of a philosophy must be mea- sured culturally and historically in terms of the phil- osophy's relevance to a particular moral environment" (p. 470).

Because philosophies are personally created and "culturally conditioned and oriented" their attractiveness to a generational or geographic audience is a variable independent of their validity. Witness, among a plethora of possible examples, the example already cited of Analytic epistemologists who appeal to and use Santayana's distinction between the reasons for and the causes of an action, while refusing to read him. The philosopher-scientist Whitehead, on the other hand, thought that Santayan would, because he was so readable, continue to have an influence beyond that of his contemporaries.

Schneider adds something to this distinction between the validity (assertive, exhibitive or active validity) and the circumstanced value of a philosophy:

"Whatever the validity of a...system, its value depends on circumstances. And no philosopher can... admit that the value of his ideas is not for him an essential consideration, for if he be indifferent to values he cannot pretend to have a philosophy."

It is because philosophers are transmitters of values that other predicates than "true" or "false" must be applied to them, as Schneider said at the beginning of the article quoted, and it is for this reason that historians of philosophy do in fact apply other predi- cates to the philosophies they review.

The Funding of Experience

"Historical being" for Schneider is a fundamental dimension of "cultural being." Of course, "natural happenings continually intrude on the course of human operations (which are the immediate subject of history) ..." "But admitting this," Schneider continues (WB p. 54f.), "we do not admit that human history is a chapter in natural history...and that historical explanation is the same as physical explanation." Eschewing the polemics that his twofold assertion might have started in an epistemological audience of 1962, Schneider concentrated on explicating his conception of historical being as "the funding of experience." [Ways of Being was, indeed, the seventh set of triennial "Woodbridge Lectures" initiated at Columbia University in 1940-1941.]

According to Schneider, where nature admits no such divisions, history is conventionally divided into past, present and future "times." Of these "only the present is in operation" (WB p. 56). But in human experience and culture the present "is dependent on having a past....It must carry its historical past with it into the future, and this `living' past in the present is...what has been...funded for reference and recall when needed."

This is why "historical composition must be up-to-date, continually reshaping its perspectives to a changing present":

"all of us...need a bigger and better past as our present. Or...as a French existentialist warns us, we are being robbed of our future because so much of our past is meaningless for the narrow present...."

Consider an example from recent history of philosophy: the supersedence in "The Home University Library of Modern Knowledge" of Laird's Recent Philosophy (1936, 1945) by Warnock's English Philosophy Since 1900 (1958, 1961). In a disingenuous Preface to the latter Warnock denies that he is being historical or that he is making a personal contribution to philosophy. Observably, however, Warnock is both reconstructing the past of philosophy and seeking, at the expense of one set of thinkers in whom he is not interested, to validate (by exhibiting them) the views of another set of thinkers in whom he is interested. The effective sense in which Warnock's book is not historical is that in which, rather than qualify Laird's previous reconstruction of the past, or add to it, Warnock silently tries to replace it. This is the sense in which it is destructive rather than reconstructive, ideological rather than historical.

The task of history, in Schneider's words, is to build, maintain and use the past intelligently not ideologically. He insisted that the "intelligent funding of human experience" calls for imagination as much as anything else. Observation of how men anticipate the future made him see that

"It is impossible to possess a future in any significant...sense without possessing a mature past. Consciousness...having a full present is precisely the interplay of past and future, the bringing together of the learned and to-be-lived.... `Having a mind' and `being historical' are therefore two ways of describing the same fact of experience."

Being imaginative about the future, or being historical about it, is not the same as being nomological: "even the most carefully funded past is only an approximate guide to the future." It is hard to see how, on the empirical grounds they profess to find decisive, the nomologists themselves could disagree with Schneider when it is a question of the sociopolitical or economic future of groups and individuals. An interesting byproduct of Schneider's carefulness, here, is the insight into what it is that determines the quality of the present in the kind of society in which we live (WB p. 58):

"What is ahead of us is what our heads are full of, and without this imagination of what is to be, the.. becoming present of the future would have no excitement in it. The disparity between what comes to be and what was supposed to become is what keeps the mind alive and incites interest. This gamble in historical existence...is known among metaphysicians by the more dignified name of contingency."

Schneider had said, in The Puritan Mind (1930 p.3f.) "past and present are...alike mysterious, but... they nevertheless make each other intelligible." In that book he had been concerned that "a world of thought [which] is slowly created...[like] the mental world of New England...may perish overnight," because of the great rift between the assumptions of our great grand-parents and our own. At the same time he felt that such rifts "make a history of the mental life of a people almost as impossible as unprofitable." Here Schneider has simultaneously pinpointed both the need for and the difficulty of intellectual history.

The solution which he found for the problem of intellectual history was based on his recognition,

first, that "the arts are not surplus products of life;
they are rather life's very essence" (PM p. 5).
Secondly, if we are "to understand why these flights
[of religion and philosophy] appeared to afford wider
perspectives and fresh points of vantage for the lives
out of which they arose," the difficulty must be
undertaken in a "spirit of _imaginative_ adventure."
Thirdly, because philosophies are such that men live
and die within them, because they are not disembodied
contributions to knowledge (PM p.6), the intellectual
historian must be concerned with the biographical facts
of "the lives and deaths of famous ideas."

Fourthly, because no living thing can feed only on
itself, "nor do ideas grow out of the mind," to be able
to understand the origin and import of an idea "one
must examine the teeming world by which it was
generated and into which it falls." By their import
Schneider meant, not their dialectical correlation to
some desocialized abstractions esconced in somebody's
anatomical museum of skeletal forms, but their temporal
meanings to those who held them "and in whose lives
they played a living part." For Schneider "a living
ideal is understood when seen in terms of its
environment." In contrast, the anatomical dissection of
it can be no more than instrumental to the study of the
living functions it served.

Looking back at Schneider's philosophic and historical achievement, we can now see that his success in
characterizing basic themes of N. American thought,
from puritanism and transcendentalism to evolutionism
and pragmatism, has depended not only on his creative
doubts and philosophic ability but also, and basically,
on the methodological insistence that to neglect the
circumstantial background and social habitat of ideas
is to put the living functions and working natures of
ideas beyond the reach of good understanding.

Philosophy, History and System

It is worth remarking that J.H. Randall's (1899-1981) conception of the cultural function of philosophy (PAI 1942, p. 25-36) is not very different from Levi-Strauss's idea about the role of myths in mediating the intellectual tensions of a society, and reconciling needed but incompatible beliefs of the society ("The Structural Study of Myth" 1955, in MAS p. 50-66).

According to the anthropologist myths mediate otherwise irreconcilable beliefs in a less self-conscious manner than philosophy, namely, in a narrative, dramatic or imagistic way. Levi-Strauss's structuralist point is that this is how given oppositions can be held in suspension and, thus, be tolerated by the society. According to Randall a "defining characteristic" of "modern philosophy" has been its persistent concern with "the fundamental conflict between two types of knowledge, one of ancient repute and one...being born ...The fact of knowledge...presents a central...problem...when two conflicting types of knowledge are struggling for men's allegiance. And this has been the case since Aristotelian science entered in the twelfth century to compete with the tradition of Christian...truth ....until the acceptance...of an enlarged and deepened...scientific method....But with the rise on every hand of dogmatic social gospels...and of sophisticated versions of a special religious 'truth,' it seems likely that 'modern philosophy' will come to a new birth" (CP 1962 p. 13f.).

Out of his concern for the human quality of the social process Randall could have added that modern philosophy is also called upon to mediate between "scientific" knowledge in the cognitivist-theoretical and "applied science" senses, on one hand, and political and ethical knowledge in the "ecosystematic" and "emancipatory" or humanizing senses on the other. Besides seeking to limit, by non-coercive means, the uses of the former kind of knowledge to human uses, the latter kind of judgment adduces emerging values in need of recognition or recovery and new perceptions requiring articulation, as the problematic basis and context of the pursuit of both useful and theoretic knowledge.

Randall's earlier statement in the pages which he wrote of _Philosophy: An Introduction_ (1942) to the effect that philosophy is the intellectual phase of cultural change, now seems too general (pp. 2, 22,

35f.). Philosophy is not all of the intellectuality of a time, nor yet of its spirituality, unless we stipulate that the "philosophy" of a culture will mean just that: the intellectuality and spirituality of a time. If by intellectually Randall meant "discursively systematic," and if by "systematic" he meant something broader than "logically systematic" but still assertive (in Buchler's sense of assertive judgment), then this is not broad enough. On the Aristotelian view that the Latinate "intellectual" means "dianoetic," philosophy is just one kind of expression or construction among others in the cultural process. Music and the plastic arts, literature and the special sciences are all, also, dianoetic processes--not to mention the politics and legislation, the therapies and religions of a culture.

However, when we see that the emphasis is on "the process by which conflicts within a culture are analysed and clarified, resolved and composed" and on philosophy "as the method of criticizing and reorganizing beliefs," we also see that Randall and Buchler believe that "the...problems of adjusting different ideas to each other" are "philosophic" problems. Suggestive too is their analogy between this process and "the political problem of adjusting different ways of acting." But a demurrer is needed, namely, that "ideas" may have been taken by Randall to refer to abstracted, verbalized ideas or ideas not needing embodiment. This would exclude ideas articulated in media other than the medium of assertive judgment, such as plastic or musical ideas as well as ideas which are acted out in or by the culture. When this sort of ideas is included, as in Buchler's subsequent systematic work, philosophy is no longer limited to discussing only verbalizations of the ideas advanced by action or the arts, but may and should itself attempt to articulate what it finds in action or the arts in any mode it pleases. On this demurrer we can concur with the finding that:

"It is because the starting-point of his [the philosopher's as statesman of ideas] enterprise is the adjustment of tensions and conflicts that the history of philosophy is best understood in terms of its analytic function, of problems of method, rather than in terms of its speculative function, of their culmination and fruit in imaginative vision. And that is why also the method of philosophic criticism and reconstruction, though always... intimately bound up with the prevalent 'scientific method,' is

71

never...exhausted in it, but always retains something of the art of the politician of the mind" (p.
35).

[Of _Philosophy: An Introduction_ Ch. I, Part I was
mainly by Randall. Buchler wrote Parts II and III of
the book with the exception of some four pages.
(Personal communication to the author by Justus
Buchler.) Buchler in 1942 had still to produce his
systematic critique and formulation of the metaphysics
of experience and judgment, nature and method,
possibility and actuality.]

Another respect in which Randall's conception of
the succession of philosophies is parallel to Levi-
Strauss's account of myths, helps to clarify Randall's
view of what he calls a philosophic tradition in _How
Philosophy Uses Its Past_. This is the respect in which
every myth is taken by Levi-Strauss to consist of all
its variants or reinterpretations (MAS p. 51-64).

Clearly, only endogenic reinterpretations are
intended by Levi-Strauss. Clarification is needed because on one hand, for Randall as for Schneider, the
aims of philosophic thinking change radically with the
generations. "What have we in common," Randall says,
"with the intellectual difficulties of our grandfa-
thers' generation, now incredibly remote?... The philosophic problems of one age, like the cultural conflicts
out of which they take their rise, are irrelevant to
those of another" (CP p. 7). But on the other hand,
Randall sees the _history_ of sets of philosophic ideas
as "both _cumulative_ and original" (CP p. 10 my emphases). Randall's language is a bit careless here, he
says "ideas" when he means "sets of related ideas." The
reader will see in HPUP that what Randall affirms about
sets of ideas here, is denied of unit-ideas there.
Clarification is also needed because, as Schneider
reminds us, philosophies are not cumulative in the
sense that the theoretical sciences are (PCA p. 467ff.
and PM p. 3-7).

Individual philosophies are either original or
reinterpretive or both. It is philosophic traditions--
in so far as they undergo adaptive modifications at the
hands of their devotees or internal reorganization,
explication and extension from within--which are cumulative. In so far as philosophy as a whole, according to
Randall, is cumulative it is so in a way different from
this. It is cumulative only of some serviceable dist-

inctions which, when taken as tools by thinkers outside
the tradition that originated them, acquire lives of
their own as "they" are applied, on new premises, to
new subject-matters or in a different context.

Consider some examples from practice which try to
give content to Randall's idea. In Aristotle's distinction between matter (hylē) and form (morphē) it is
not possible for the referents of each term in the
distinction to exist separately or pure. Under the
influence of pythagorism, neoclassicism and the rationalism of the Hellenistic and medieval world, the distinction was distorted in the direction of formalism and
applied as a distinction between substance (Lat. sub-
stantia) and form (forma). Thus where for Aristotle
matter had been the substrate (hypokeimenon; Lat. sub-
iectus, suppositus), form, in becoming primary among
Neoplatonists and Scholastics, acquired separate and
independent existence. Because the distinction so modified gives support to idealist and supernaturalist
theses, materialists and physicalists reacted by taking
matter as primary and independent without noticing that
what they were calling matter was never pure matter or,
else, a physicist's construct. What they were calling
matter was, in fact, what Aristotle had called _ousia_
(being, substance) because it was always matter _infor-
med_ in some way. We have to say that it is not the same
distinction at all, or that the distinction between
matter and form was redrawn as a biased distinction
with novel systematic consequences. And these consequences contradict each other, depending on which term of
the biased distinction is given more importance or
ontological priority.

Again, it is demonstrable that the different uses
made of the distinction between appearance and reality
by F.H. Bradley, the objective realist, and B. Russell,
the physicalist, turn the distinction into a different
one for each of them. In Bradley the distinction is
part of a relativism that tries to be pluralist about
existence and about what is good. In Russell the distinction is part of a relativism on which he bases his
positivist priorities and his defiant but inadequate
humanism; it is, in several respects, more like the
distinction between illusion and reality.

The overdrawn distinction favored by Eighteenth
century neoclassicists between aisthēsis and noēsis
(sensation and thought) is not a distinction at all in
the original Parmenides, despite his commentator Sim-

plicius. And it is a different distinction in the original Aristotle from that found among the modern philosophers, whether rationalist or empiricist, realist or nominalist. In so far as the latter distinct philosophic traditions do use the same distinction between aisthēsis and noēsis, it is because they share some presuppositions about art which cut across their otherwise opposed philosophies. The shared presuppositions and defective perceptions about art became common to the two schools because they had come to constitute an underlabelled tradition of talking about art which made no systematic difference to the opposition of the two schools.

Is it not then only such labels as realism, rationalism, physicalism etc., which we all use and can easily monitor for ambiguity, that remain equally applicable by philosophers in differing traditions? But this is a sociohistorical use of terms or distinctions, in something like the sense intended by Randall. So it is the history of philosophy, or better, philosophic histories which are cumulative not philosophy as a whole.

In short, if we take examples of such distinctions as each constituting one complex idea, we find that in the history of philosophy a complex idea which recurrs in differing philosophers under the same label, is not the same idea at all. We conclude that what Randall says in How Philosophy Uses Its Past (p.54-55) about the artificiality of Lovejoy's conception of unit-ideas, applies to his own notion of perennially usable distinctions. [A more extended critique of Lovejoy's conception can be found in my "The Human Sciences in Dewey, Foucault and Buchler," The Southern Journal of Philosophy XVIII, 2 (1980).] It is only within a given tradition and its presuppositions that such ideas or distinctions, which I call connotational clusters, do not lose their identity. We see that Randall, the diligent philosophic historian, has momentarily confused philosophy with the history of philosophy.

Human Reagents in Cultural Change

As a productive critic who identified equally with the enterprise of philosophy and the enterprise of history, Randall believed that the practice of insightful philosophic history requires the formulating of a philosophy of cultural change (CP p. 7). This is because (i) "The history of human thought, and the history of philosophical ideas in particular, exhibits with unusual clarity the general structure of social and cultural change," and because (ii) "the great philosophies...that have seen beyond their special problems of adjustment and partisan loyalty, though they speak in different languages, seem...to be speaking of the same universal structure of experience."

Randall is suggesting not only that the ability to produce good intellectual history, or history of philosophy, involves the ability to do good philosophy but that something philosophically valuable can be learned from good history of ideas. The implication is that to be good a philosophy must, like good art, address the human condition at some level that transcends the limitations of circumstance and partisanship. Randall outlines his own philosophy of cultural change in Nature and Historical Experience. The associated claim that "history brings philosophical understanding" is developed both in the latter and in How Philosophy Uses Its Past.

Resurveying cultural developments in terms of "focal problems" in the changing society, Randall concluded that there have always been four main kinds of parties to cultural change. There are, first, the basically indifferent, those who have to be won over, the drifters who "are the raw material of change." --Notice that Randall, like Plato's Socrates in the Gorgias and Phaedrus, believes that persons are the proper targets or "raw materials" of the art of philosophic reconception. The difference with Plato's Socrates is that Socrates saw philosophic reconception as part of the true art of rhetoric.-- Randall cites as an example of cultural drift, how the substance of education came to be lost in recent American history as it was replaced by a mere faith in education. This faith was all that the drifters were able to retain, and institutionalize, from the activists' innovative attempts to make formal education both more functional (more easily usable) and more widespread (interesting to more people) in the society.

The second kind of party to cultural change are the partisans of the new idea being proposed as the solution to a new central problem. Randall calls these the radicals and the reactionaries; they are partisans of regressive solutions, extremists of opposed sorts who nonetheless resemble each other in some respects. He chooses two examples likely to give offense to both sets of opposed partisans: "Thus logical positivists are if anything more dogmatic than metaphysicians--not to mention the many resemblances between Communists and Catholics" (CP p. 105). We have to say that emotion generated by the examples is a sure sign that the quarrels involved are far from over. And we note that Randall cited them in 1958, before the Catholics of Poland had found non-extremist ways of reacting against the extremism of Soviet communism.

A history is always an account of a change from some determinate tendency. It points to what will happen in the future if the tendency is not modified, if the problems it is seen to present are not addressed. Partisans find, consequently, that the solutions they support are impeded both by the facts of practice and the internal logic of the ideas they oppose (CP p. 102f.). But neither does the society see all the implications of the new or revived ideas which the partisans are, respectively, supporting.

"Thus," says Randall, "'evolution' meant at first primarily a...substitute for Providence; and only later were its more revolutionary intellectual bearings realized." Thus, too, many partisans of Hutchins' restoration of "the great books" to a central place in education did not see the anti-creative possibilities of the movement: the great books, it came to be implied, have all been written, the rest is commentary. Nor did other adherents foresee the progressive deterioration of the idea lurking in the substitution of great time-tested books with great untested books which were only greatly attractive or greatly fashionable in some circles. [There are obscurities in Randall's prose on these pages, perhaps because it is not clear whether his account takes the historian's point of view of the society as a whole, or the point of view of the mediators who constitute the fourth kind of party to cultural change. Randall's allusion to Hutchins the anti-historical educator is not accompanied by any analysis.]

76

On the basis of this inductive, but also interpretive, analysis of recurrent roles waiting to be filled by the participants in cultural change, Randall states that "the pattern illustrated by each conflict and solution remains pretty much the same...it is a pattern we can be fairly sure our own conflicts will follow" (CP p. 7). At least two comments can be made about this claim to have found a recurrent pattern in the way succeeding intellectual conflicts run through their cycles.

Throughout the discussion of this pattern in NHE, CP and HPUP Randall does not distinguish enough between conflicts among philosophies themselves and conflicts in the society which the philosophies may reflect or express. What he says seems to apply to conflicts of value and ideology in the society at large rather than to conflicts among philosophies. And do all intellectual conflicts in the society get reflected in the philosophies of their times and, if reflected, reflected as conflicts?

We have already referred, for example, to the agreement between Rationalists and Empiricists of the seventeenth and eighteenth centuries on the subject of art, and the subject of perception in relation to art. This strange agreement can be seen to have blocked the reflection, by philosophy, of the endemic conflict in Baroque and Augustan Europe between artists and craftsmen, on one hand, and scientists and philosophers on the other. In this conflict not only was the value of art downgraded or distorted; the intellectual validity of art as a kind of intelligent construction and expression was denied or suppressed.--As an artist who succeeded in making himself a social exception to the conflict, the best Joshua Reynolds could do for art was to re-use the neoplatonist notion that art somehow turns the contemplation of concrete particulars into insight about the universals which it is "copying." This move is insufficient to letimate art as cognitive gain, or to account for the kinds of deep meaningfulness which great art offers. By abetting domination of the theoretical over the sensible, Reynolds' neoclassicism must only have hastened the Romantic reaction.

Secondly, in the case of the philosophic conflict between the tradition to which Randall belongs and the school of linguistic analysis and neopositivism, it was the latter that looked like a new radicalism. Randall himself had been, at first, a _radical_ of the new demo-

cratic and labor humanism and, later, a _mediator_ between the idea of scientific knowledge as the new
enterprise of our civilization and the idea of religion
as a continuing need of the individual and society.
[For the record, Randall's Ph.D. thesis reflects his
sympathies: _The Problem of Group Responsibility to
Society_. An Interpretation of the History of American
Labor (Columbia University 1922).] Furthermore, the
self-styled Analytic philosophy and neopositivism that
displaced Randall's philosophic tradition avoided
acknowledging that tradition as even a party to their
quarrel. They rather took phenomenologists, existentia-
lists, neomarxists and religious humanists as their
opposition. But a good number of all these have not, in
fact, been appealing too _old_ solutions as Randall's
pattern specifies.

The historical fact would seem to be, rather, that
the innovations of the non-positivist, historical expe-
rientialism of American philosophy--with its notions of
a humanist religion and of a science in service to
humanity--had not found the kind of support in the
culture which could have helped it resist the bureau-
cratic onslaught of the fashion for simplifying logical techniques. The latter gave a quickly acquired sense
of mastery and certainty to converts faced with a
tangle of inherited conflicts, precisely because of the
historical blindness of logistic analysis and the dog-
matism it masks as a set of purely formal distinctions.

The weakness of Randall's generalizing about intellectual history is, perhaps, due to the fact that he
could not imagine that such philosophic gains as those
made by Peirce's methodological pragmaticism, by
James's redefinition of philosophy as the pursuit of
reflective clarity, by Dewey's regrounding of metaphysics in process and function, of aesthetics in experience and of ethics in the continuum of means and ends,
could ever again be bypassed by serious thinkers or
removed from the tool-kit of philosophy. For, these
were gains definitive of the very tradition within
which Randall had developed and worked. But they _were_
bypassed by philosophies imported from abroad in and
after the decade of 1950. And some of these gains of
classic American philosophy are only now beginning to
be recovered. It remains to be seen whether they will
be recovered as the same gains, as the same sort of
philosophic insights, or as transformed distinctions.

Thus, what remains of Randall's pattern, when

78

tested historically against the example of his own philosophy and its antagonists is (i) that philosophies often reflect major blindnesses in the culture and not all the conflicts in it, (ii) that philosophic schools, though they reflect opposed trends, may side-step the opposition instead of facing it. Where, for example, G.E. Moore and B. Russell had tried to refute British idealism (PS 1922; TPP 1913), Warnock simply ignores it (EPSN 1958); while American converts to Viennese neopositivism and British analyticism acted as if they did not know that many of "their" own theses, such as verificationism, or philosophy as reflective clarity, or instrumentalism were already on the books in usable or modulatable form.

Randall's pattern is true to historical experience, thirdly, mainly in so far as the pattern says that, in the process of intellectual change, there will always be some who are drifters and some who are extremists in either some regressive or progressive sense. The pattern is also correct in projecting that there will always be mediators. But it seems to me that there is no guarantee that these will be mediating the most deep-seated or urgent conflicts. And there is no guarantee that the mediators will not be taken, for their efforts, as polemicists of some one of the extremes by those of another. Fourthly, we are confirmed in our doubt that while philosophy in its traditionary parts may be cumulative, philosophy as a whole is not.

What Distinguishes History of Philosophy from Philosophy

The very opposite of the common run of philosophers who practice philosophy unhistorically and history of philosophy unreflectively, Randall was reflective about regular histories, as in his essay in the cooperative volume on The Theory and Practice of Historical Study (1943). In contrast to the presumptuous naivete about historical studies of some recent philosophic theorizing about history, Randall's example could be taken as a paradigm of what the relationship should be between a reflective historian of philosophy and historical study.

Randall loved, and was involved in, the subject of social and intellectual history as much as any historian. His essays attest to this, while his full and illuminating The Making of the Modern Mind (1926; rev. 1940) remains required reading to this day. Philosophers who cannot learn from the example of Randall because his views are too different give evidence, thereby, that they lack the inclusive pluralism that is a condition of the best histories. Thinkers who practice philosophic history with exclusionary results, whether deliberately or not, should worry that it is a characteristic of sheer belief-communities (as opposed to scientific communities) that they hold exclusionary beliefs, and that they do not admit beliefs that, on their own criteria of acceptability, they might admit.

It is not an accident that Randall's analysis of "Controlling Assumptions in the Practice of American Historians" (TPHS 1946) is applicable, in its generalizable conclusions, to the practice of the history of philosophy. This is because reflective history of philosophy is a distinctive kind of history as well as a kind of conceptual analysis and because, if it is to include what it must include to be history (not just polemical analysis), it cannot avoid getting into a dialectical relationship with philosophies that might be alien to the philosophy of the historian himself.

By dialectical relationship is meant an open interlocutory stance which can enter into the generative assumptions of the explicit claims in the philosophies he must give an account of. Only so will the philosophic historian be able to give an internal critique of the system whose development or succession he is concerned with. But to get understanding of the generative premises of an alien system, the historian will have to bring into consideration the sociohistorical context, the intellectual aims and other motivations of the system. By an internal critique is meant, precisely, a reflective exposition which supplies the reader with the unstated (but possible) assumptions that must be made in order to make sense of unpalatable claims or to restore to the alien system the coherence which it must have had for its defenders.

The first point Randall makes in "Controlling Assumptions" (TPHS) is that historians cannot avoid being selective about what is to count as basic in their histories. If the principle of selection can change with time, for a particular historian of a given subject-matter--as it did for Charles Beard in his two histories of the United States-- it should not surprise us that differnet schools and generations of historians will have different principles of selection. And this will be not only because the historians' assumptions and outlook have changed, but because

> "there is...something different to understand. The history-that-has-happened, has been progressive and cumulative...Hence the historian, facing the problem of selecting those facts in the...past that seem `basic' for 1944, will not be able to make just the same selection he made in 1927" (TPHS p. 18).

It follows that the duty of the philosophic historian will be to make as explicit as he can the principles of selection he is using in the organization of his subject-matter. The philosopher who, like Warnock in the example cited earlier (EPSN), does not do this invites serious charges. He invites the charge that he is ignorant of what he has omitted or that he is dissimulating his partisanship or that he is incapable of philosophic self-reflection or that he is claiming that what he has omitted were not problems, or that there is no problem about omitting without mention ideas that were previously prevalent.

For Randall, philosophic history needs to be rewritten because "our understanding of [intellectual] consequences changes with the working out of further consequences in the history-that-happens itself" (TPHS p. 19). The society's understanding of what is determinative of philosophic change also changes or becomes controversial. And, whether he can settle controversies or not, the business of the historian and philosopher is not to silence controversy but to recognize it and report on it.

It is the historian's sense of the future, combined with his understanding of the present, that helps him to decide what sets of problems are _now_ basic in the past, recent or remote. On Randall's functionalist approach, the meaning of an idea or set of ideas is to be found in its effects or what it does. In line with this, the importance of a complex of ideas or problems will vary as the philosopher's understanding of the present varies, and as his sense of the future changes. In the case of the philosophic historian, the principles of selection would be philosophically held only if they are not arbitrary and if reasons are given for his choice of them and the way he applies them. For example, says Randall (TPHS p. 21),

"to take the growth of science as the basic factor in the intellectual history of modern times, means that we judge it to be of most significance today."

But were the example to be asserted as a commitment, today's intellectual historian would have to revise it to say that it is the insufficiently controlled growth of technological applications of research-science that has become a basic factor in the intellectual life of the present. And this means that we judge this lack of control, by reference either to physical science itself or to the democracy at large, to be of the greatest significance for our future. We have to add that, though good theoretical-experimental science and well-functioning democracy provide ways of lessening arbitrariness, Randall is too optimistic when he says "practical knowledge of what has to be done, like technical knowledge of how to do it is relatively free from the `arbitrariness' and irresponsible `relativism'" of mere ideologues and idea-mongers (TPHS p. 22). The numerous instances of unsafe nuclear engineering for peaceful purposes, the unsolved problem of nuclear waste-disposal and the continuing production of nuclear overkill, demonstrate that while instrumental (means-end) knowledge may be non-arbitrary _within_ technology, "practical [praxical] knowledge of what has to be done" _with_ technology is not only difficult to come by and get acceptance for, but is essentially controversial. As politics, and like politics, practical judgment only becomes less arbitrary as citizen assent is less coerced and as participation becomes more informed and

82

representation more effective in the human interest.

It is indeed "in terms of...ends that have to be achieved...goals forced on us by facts" that "men understand the present and the past, using these ends as principles for selecting what is basic in the histories they write" (TPHS p. 22). But were the historian's or philosopher's selection to be based merely on what is important for him, his history or philosophy would be subjective and arbitrary. Contrariwise, a publicly verifiable or discussable focus on something to be done or avoided will be non-private and falsifiable, i.e. objective. Such objectivity is the knowledgeable precondition for facing problems in terms of the conditions within which they arose, of considering the means to their solution and perceiving the course of what is actually happening. It is the possession of a full relational context of conditions and consequences, means and ends that permits objectivity about past and present and that unmasks unmonitored emphases as ideological, sectarian or arbitrarily precommitted.

When we observe that so many standard histories of philosophy do not make explicit some or any of the selective principles behind their emphases and interpretations, we have to reject the practice as unphilosophic because it is lacking in self-reflectiveness. Such histories, like some philosophies, are simply exempting themselves from the criteria of reflectiveness which they apply to others. They often also find it convenient to apply their criteria for the use of evidence, and their method of text interpretation, on the basis of unstated philosophic preferences insufficiently examined. In so far as this denatures the relevant literary evidence and texts, and in so far as it creates "evidence" by sheer consensus, it could not be more unhistorical or anti-historical.

Thus, as idealists with an unexamined preference for "system," German historians from Heinrich Ritter, Ueberweg and Zeller to Wilamowitz and Friedlaender could only see Plato's series of differently designed dialogues as an idealist system in disguise. Had they been self-critical, they might have been able to see that what they were talking about was not Plato's multi-faceted dialogical works but an Academic and neoplatonist tradition of discourse which had made habitual the practice of quoting--out of context and without identification--lines from speeches by characters confronting or prompting each other under the very particular determining circumstances instituted by each dialogue. This is uncritical both as history and as philosophy and represents, in would-be scholars such as Constantin Ritter and A.E. Taylor, a nadir in Plato studies from which philosophic history has yet to emerge.

On the other hand and by exception, the example of Joseph Owens' study of Aristotle's influence (DBAM 1951) is neither unhistorical nor unphilosophical, because it is clear from the first that what is being dealt with is the "Aristotelian" metaphysics of the Latin tradition, and because Owens makes no mystery of his own interests or principles. On the other side, E. Buchanan's Aristotle's _Theory_ _of_ _Being_ is historical and philosophic, because it explicitly avoids the Latin reconceptualization of the key Greek terms in Aristotle's metaphysics.

About the standard unhistorical histories of philosophy the careful reader concludes with dismay that what makes them look distinctive, as opposed to general histories or intellectual histories, is not so much their subject-matter as their lack of historical conscientiousness. That a literary historian can hold his own philosophically, in comparison with standard histories of philosophy, is shown by Leslie Stephen's _English_ _Thought_ _in_ _the_ _Eighteenth_ _Century_. Though philosophers' histories do seem to treat their subject-matter more reflectively than philological histories, they must still be said to fail in reflectivenss where they are unhistorical. In the latter case, the quality of reflection in the philosophers is subverted by their insensitivity to the literary-historical and philological (linguistic) dimensions of the texts. In the case of the idealist historians cited above, their philological interest was not matched by their literary sensitivity. And the underdevelopment of philosophic skill nurtured by adherence to orthodoxy kept them from suspecting that something might be philosophically wrong with a concept according to which--in the study of Plato--an idealist system was being advanced by means of dialogues which wittily satirize idealism when they mention or use it. Or that something might be wrong with a method that treats brilliant conversational interactions as catechical tracts in which the order of the supposedly systematic questions is undecidable and in which the questioner is sometimes the answerer, or sometimes contradicts himself from dialogue to dialogue, or is sometimes contradicted by other leading speakers in the dialogues.

What makes philosophic history of philosophy distinctive, then, is not the fact that it takes a number of philosophic systems for its subject-matter. For, this is not enough to make it history, as C.E.M. Joad knew when he called his own works "Guides To" philosophy or moral philosophy (GP 1935, GMP 1938). Nor does the chronology of artificially abstracted "unit-ideas" qualify as either good philosophy or good history. Unit-ideas are lexicographer's artifacts which denature the connotational complexes that the history of ideas is supposed to sort out. This is because a connotational cluster cannot properly be understood except in terms of the function it served in its sociohistorical and axiological environment (HPUP, HSDFB). Semantic or connotational changes in idea-complexes can be kept under experiential control only if their relation to denotational and intentional circumstances is retraced and identified.

Thus, to be _history_, history of ideas must be sociohistorically circumstantial and axiologically contextual. And, if it is to deal with intellectual realities rather than artifacts, it must analyze idea-complexes in the contexts of their effectiveness as parts of a social world and as parts of what Randall calls an intellectual tradition. For, it is the traditions that are the real units in the history of philosophy or the history of culture.

To be philosophic as well, histories of philosophy must deal non-reductively and analytically with the systems and sets of ideas which are their subject-matter. As a critique of validly identified connotational clusters, philosophic reflection cannot always avoid seeming polemical. But if it is fully, or doubly, reflective in the sense that it monitors its own presuppositions and methods as well as those of its subjects, then the critique will be dialectical rather than polemical. It will have engaged the deepest premises of properly understood distinctions and conceptions within the generative matrix of their tradition, and in contrast to explicit not hidden alternative matrices.

But a plea to philosophers to be historical when they do history of philosophy, and a reminder that they are assuming some history when they think they are being only philosophical, will not be effective unless it is also shown that history brings understanding. So, this is what Randall undertakes to do in the last chapter of HPUP, "How History Brings Philosophical Understanding."

Philosophy , for Randall, has to be seen as "the intellectual reaction of outstanding minds to other...culturally significant events" in the sciences, the arts and the society (p.73). Otherwise, the pointedness of its critique will be missed or muted. "The history of philosophical ideas...helps to make clear what our available ideas....have been, and what they have been able so far to do" for us (p. 74). In so far as a philosophic generation has developed new ideas and new methods, it should certainly use them. But if philosophers trained in new methods have no historical perspective on the problems outstanding, they will fail to perceive that these are often only inherited problems and not "the intellectual difficulties that insistently confront us" (p. 75). It is not only the application of a new method that dissolves an old problem into a mere puzzle. Old questions or issues also cease to be relevant as the result of historical change. Having ceased to be relevant or central, a problem will no longer be one; and will, indeed, have come to look like an intellectual curiosity or puzzle. Thus, says Randall,

"It is not only the analysis of language that can prove emancipating and therapeutic. Historical knowledge is the greatest of all liberators from the mistakes and muddles, from the tyranny of the past."

Because of the senses in which the special sciences are not self-reflective, philosophy of science will always "be interpreting the scientist's changing enterprise to the scientist himself, not merely to the layman." But this necessary job of interpretation cannot be done without knowledge of the history of the sciences, or on the uncritical basis of some single preferred model of what "science" is. As "a process of criticism, ever renewed, of the ideas men are using" to solve pressing problems, philosophy is not cumulative (in the senses already specified). But if they are going to be critical "philosophers cannot with impunity make a completely `fresh start.' Rather to make their start effective, they...usually have to go back to the `beginning,' to examine just where the incompleteness or inadequacy of an idea came from and how to modify it" (p. 80). Moreover, the philosopher--like the scientist in this respect--should know the field (here, some sciences) before he can be conceptually innovative about it (p. 79). But in every special area of philosophy, "the field" always consists of sets of contrastable traditions about the way distinctions are made or taken, and about how the data of the special sciences and the lore of the culture are to be interpreted.

As a historian Randall notes that the reaction in philosophy against the historical interest was part of a reaction, in some places, against the Hegelian philosophy and its claim to be the historical culmination of Western philosophic thought. In other places, and after World War II, anti-history was a reaction against the fact that "philosophy was taken... as the [historical] development of the scheme of intelligibility that is science, in the teachings of... Brunschvig, Meyerson and Koyre" (p. 83). It follows that what was really rejected were schemes of intelligibility by thinkers with new schemes of intelligibility. And philosophic history suffered the consequences of having been so heavily invoked as evidence for the finality of the rejected schemes. But the ensuing neglect of philosophic history constituted only another kind of abuse, not a correction of the previous one. Philosophic history, we perceive, must be broken of the tempting habit of letting itself be used to buttress the validity or finality of a philosophy as a system of truth-claims.

The store of extant philosophic systems and traditions does, indeed, become more usable when these are seen as more than the practice of ideas. When seen as "the poetry of ideas" (p. 85f.) and as "the record of intellectual experiments" showing "where certain methods and assumptions have led...and the impasses they have confronted" (p. 78ff.), philosophic traditions no longer need refutation. To Randall's historical observation every great philosopher has studied previous philosophers in other traditions. "The Greeks, we say, were happy in having a diversity of traditions on which to draw" (p. 88).

> "The major philosophers have been quite aware that no original mind can afford to cut the ties that link him with the great thinkers of his past. Each such towering figure has felt the compulsion to come to terms with his `predecessors."

Here, the examples would be Plato and Aristotle who represent the second stage and pre-foundations of the

Western traditions, and who give so much evidence of having studied their predecessors.

But Randall is also aware that in going to their predecessors for hypotheses, suggestions and insights to build upon, "they do not prize highly historical accuracy." Thus "Whitehead had a genius for finding in earlier thinkers ideas no one had ever...suspected were hidden there" (p. 88). Nonetheless the benefit that this brings to philosophers is "liberat[ion]...from the provinciality of their own tradition." Randall celebrates the fact that, until the early 'Sixties at least,

"American philosophizing has been fortunate in its freedom from this limitation to a single national tradition: the insularism of the British, the provinciality of the French, the self-containedness of the German. American philosophy, come of age by the end of the nineteenth century, could draw on all the different European traditions."

Practing philosophers also take their predecessors as "points of reference...on which they wish to build, or against which they wish to set off their own thinking" (p. 88).

"Those who have pushed a standpoint to the limit serve an especially useful purpose. That is why the extreme positions usually receive the strongest emphasis, and give the impression that philosophical history has been a gigantomachia, a battle of Titans, rather than a cooperative enterprise."

To feel the intellectual power of a philosophic tradition we have to study it, especially when we are anxious to go beyond it. "Else we shall find ourselves denying what it saw, instead of placing those insights in our broader context. To go beyond is to see more, not see less" (p. 89).

Historical and genetic analysis tries to ascertain just what the problems were which a past thinker was trying to solve, what the intellectual resources at his disposal were, what his assumptions were. Historical analysis also wants to have before it what the motivating interests and working assumptions of the historian himself are. In this way historical analysis can soon tell which of the past philosopher's problems were merely inherited and which were generated by living tensions about deep-seated conflicts in the culture (p. 90-93). Thus, responsible historical analysis is as convincing a method as "linguistic analysis" is claimed to be for clearing up past philosophic muddles and inherited present muddles. And it avoids the risk of mistaking a real problem, in the present or the past, for a mere semantic confusion (p. 95f.).

The historian of competing philosophic traditions will also be in a position to see that in some traditions some problems receive solutions which are better in some respects than those they get in other traditions. This perception is not only "emancipatory" or "therapeutic;" it provides a basis for making functional discriminations, among traditions, about the effectiveness with which they formulate and resolve their respective problems or cruxes. Such a historian will be able to observe the degree to which, in attacking parallel problems in their own different terms the competing traditions do interact with or influence one another.

Antipathetic as some traditions are to each other, as philosophies they are "all methods of criticizing the `abstractions' of practical common sense" and of "our formalized and systematized scientific schemes, by calling attention more adequately...to the generic traits of...the world as...encountered." In this respect competing contemporary philosophies do have problems in common, even if in different formulations and in spite of the different derivations of the philosophies. If the aim of all philosophies is "a clarification and criticism of the fundamental beliefs" of a culture "that have come into conflict" because of "fresh discover[ies]...and novel social experience[s]" (p. 100), then it is also the case that they have more in common than unhistorical members of the differing traditions believe. They may well have different "mentalities" but they will also have, up to a point, a common culture.

There is a point that Randall does not make. It is observable that contemporary members of rival traditions are more similar to each other, in given respects, than they are to the acknowledged predecessors in their own tradition. The influence, at a given historical moment, of the state of their natural languages, of the state of the arts and sciences--which states are the basis of given period styles--create deeper connections and similarities among contemporary (horizontally distributed) thinkers than those by which they are affiliated (vertically) to a school or tradition. As I see it, this is a verifiable sense in which different philosophic traditions do tend to converge, as Randall optimistically claims, in working out the implications of their different assumptions in dealing with some of the problems of their age. It may also happen that the human goals of contemporary philosophic rivals are more similar than their inherited assumptions, so that the goals occasionally and fortunately override the assumptions.

For Randall, the most impressive kind of understanding which history can bring to philosophy is the deepened and more empirical characterization or definition of philosophy itself that it permits. Clearly, an open--as opposed to partisan--characterization of philosophic activity, based on the observation of the careers and fortunes of a goodly number of philosophies in their life-cycles, will not only be a richer but also a more reliable description of what it is to philosophize than a definition which disregards the historical experience of philosophy.

Bibliography

DA 1797 J. Reynolds _Discourses_ _on_ _Art_ (Repr. N.Y. Bobbs-Merrill (1965)

HPA 1836 H. Ritter _Histoire_ _de_ _la_ _Philosophie_ _Ancienne_ 4 vols. French tr. by C.J. Tissot (Paris: Ladrange 1835-36)

PS 1839 E. Zeller _Platonische_ _Studien_ (Tuebingen: Osiander; repr. Rodopi 1969)

DPG 1844- _Die_ _Philosophie_ _der_ _Griechen_, in ihrer
     1852 geschichtlichen Entwicklung dargestellt 7 ed. 3 vols. in 6 (Leipzig 1920-23). Engl. tr., based on earlier editions, by Alleyne, Goodwin, Reichel, Costelloe, Muirhead (London: Longmans 1876-1897)

HP 1871 F. Ueberweg _History_ _of_ _Philosophy_ Vol. I, tr. G.S. Morris (N.Y. Scribner's 1871)

ETEC 1876 L. Stephens _English_ _Thought_ _in_ _the_ _Eighteenth_ Century 2 vols. (London: J. Murray; repr. 1927)

AR 1893 F.H. Bradley _Appearance_ _and_ _Reality_ (Oxford: corr. impr. 1930)

IR 1908 E. Meyerson _Identite_ _et_ _Realite_ 2 ed. 1926; tr. Loewenberg (Allen & Unwin 1930)

TPP 1913 B. Russell _The_ _Problems_ _of_ _Philosophy_ (Oxford: repr. 1946)

DES 1921 E. Meyerson _De_ _l'Explication_ _dans_ _les_ _Sciences_ (Paris: 1921)

PS 1922 G.E. Moore _Philosophical_ _Studies_ (London: Routledge)

PGRS 1922 J.H. Randall _The_ _Problem_ _of_ _Group_ _Responsibility_ _to_ _Society_ (Columbia Diss.)

PMW 1926 A.E. Taylor _Plato_. The Man and his Work (N.Y. Meridian repr. 1956)

MMM 1926 J.H. Randall _The_ _Making_ _of_ _the_ _Modern_ _Mind_ (Houghton Mifflin 2 rev. ed. 1940)

RAC   1927   C. and M. Beard The Rise of American Civilization (N.Y. Macmillan)

EPM   1929   L. Brunschvig Las Etapas de la Filosofia Matematica, tr. of the 3 ed. (Buenos Aires: Lautaro 1945; 1 Fr. ed. 1912)

PM   1930   H. Schneider The Puritan Mind (N.Y. Holt 1930; repr. Ann Arbor 1958)

EPP   1931   C. Ritter Die Kerngedanke der platonischen Philosophie tr. as The Essence of Plato's Philosophy (N.Y. Russell & Russell reprint)

GP   1935   C.E.M. Joad Guide to Philosophy (N.Y. Random House)

RP   1936   J. Laird Recent Philosophy (London: Oxf.)

GPMP   1938   C.E.M. Joad Guide to the Philosophy of Morals and Politics (N.Y. Random House)

EG   1940   A. Koyre Etudes Galileennes 3 vol. (Paris: Herman 1939; repr. 1966). Tr. J. Mepham Galileo Studies (N.J. Humanities 1978)

PAI   1942   J.H. Randall & J. Buchler Philosophy: An Introduction (N.Y. Barnes & Noble)

BHUS   1944   C. & M. Beard Basic History of the United States (N.Y. Doubleday)

HAP   1946   H. Schneider A History of American Philosophy (N.Y. Columbia)

TPHS   1946   "Controlling Assumptions in the Practice of American Historians," Theory and Practice in Historical Study (N.Y. Soc. Sci. Research Council)

NH   1950   S. Lamprecht Nature and History (N.Y. Columbia; repr. Archon 1966)

DBAM   1951   J. Owens The Doctrine of Being in the Aristotelian Metaphysics (Toronto: Pontifical Institute)

CWIU   1957   A. Koyre From the Closed World to the Infinite Universe (J. Hopkins; repr. Harper TB 1957)

EPSN   1958   G.J. Warnock English Philosophy Since 1900 (London: Oxford)

NHE   1958   J.H. Randall Nature and Historical Experience (N.Y. Columbia)

MAS   1958   C. Levi-Strauss "The Structural Study of Myth," Myth: A Symposium (Bloomington: Indiana U.)

PLW   1959   U. von Wilamowitz-Moellendorf Platon. Sein Leben und Seine Werke (Berlin: Weidmann 5 ed. 1959)

DPS   1960   P. Friedlaender Die Platonischen Schriften 3 vols. (Berlin: De Gruyter; Engl. tr. H. Meyerhoff, Bollingen 1958-60)

WB   1962   H. Schneider Ways of Being (N.Y. Columbia)

HPUP   1963   J.H. Randall How Philosophy Uses Its Past (N.Y. Columbia)

CP   1962-   J.H. Randall The Career of Philosophy 3
      1977   vols. (N.Y. Columbia 1962-1967)

PACA   1974   H. Schneider "Philosophy Will Never be a Science," Philosophy and the Civilizing Arts ed C. Walton & J. Anton (Athens: Ohio U. Press)

CAIHS   1979   V. Tejera "Cultural Analysis and Interpretation in the Human Sciences," Man and World Vol. 12, No. 2 (1979)

HSDFB   1980   V. Tejera "The Human Sciences in Dewey, Foucault and Buchler," The Southern Journal of Philosophy XVIII, 2 (1980)

IHTP   1981   V. Tejera "Intellectual History as a Tool of Philosophy," L.I.P.S. Spring 1981; in Against Antihistory in Philosophy, ed. by T. Lavine & V. Tejera (The Hague: Nijhoff t.b.a.)

Chapter V

Judgment in History

"The study of the history of our theories or ideas... should make us all pluralists."

K. Popper (OK p. 300)

Historiography and Method

In his monograph on Popper and Collingwood (MSH 1975), P. Skagestad points out that

"Popper's tenacity in linking the intellectual virtues of rationality and objectivity to the advocacy of the hypothetico-deductive method can only serve to bring those virtues in[to] discredit among those who are concerned with the human sciences" (p. 94).

I would add that it isn't only that history is an interpretive enterprise, but that all the sciences and inquiry, all judgment and query are interpretive in their different ways. We take inquiry here to be judgment in the assertive mode only; but query ranges over the domains of action (active judgment) and construction (exhibitive judgment) as well.

We saw in an earlier chapter how Buchler was able, with his notion of proception, to enlarge and make more precise the conception of "experience" found in Dewey and other philosophers. Here we will try to show how reflection can do more justice to the nature and results of the human sciences--including history--by using Buchler's reconceptions of the notions of judgment and method, than it can with the available conceptions of hypothetical-deductive method whether in Dewey or Popper (LTI 1938; PH 1957, LSD 1935).

Because, for Buchler, to have knowledge is to be able to discriminate situations in which a given judgment is applicable and required, to have a method in this sense is to have a special sort of knowledge. But there is no necessary connection, according to Buchler, between method and knowledge (ML 1974, p. 84, 149, 151).

"There are methods of acquiring knowledge, methods of suppressing knowledge, methods which yield knowledge though knowledge is not their primary aim, and methods to which the idea of knowledge is irrelevant. Looking the other way, knowledge may be ac-

95

quired methodically or non-methodically. And non-methodic knowledge may be acquired either purposively or accidently" (CM 1961, p. 116).

Since the hypothetico-deductive method cannot give a good account of the occurrence of knowing, or "cognitive gain," as part of the rationality to be found in exhibitive works (such as those of art) or in active judgments (such as those of political agents), attempts to understand histories in terms of the hypothetico-deductive method are bound to be insufficient.

As we have seen, while history-in-the-making uses many special sciences, history the product is not a social science but a construction in several dimensions. In other words, a work of history cannot be required to have the structure of a hypothetical-deductive account in some special science. This is to say, in response to Popper's way of using the terms (PDGS 1969, 87-104), that history cannot be treated as "theoretical science" only, or as only the application of theoretical science.

In response to Dewey's way of talking--which at its best tries to expand "the method of intelligence" to include the powers of the artist and statesman--histories cannot be understood as only trying to "solve problems," or as just _asserting_ something. Still, Dewey's way of taking intelligence to be the getting of control over a situation is not entirely inapt, if we think of what many histories have tried to do. But we need to specify that while it is control in the sense of "understanding" that many histories provide, the meaningfulness and renewal of the ability to act which some histories provide are also due to their exhibitive power as constructions and to the active judments which they embody and reflect.

As a methodic activity, then, history is going to embody some traits which method has in art and conduct as well as some which method has in the sciences. It is for this reason that history must be taken to be a mixed study, as stated earlier. Philosophic historiography is query in several modes because it must assess the way in which histories have used the special sciences, the way in which they have been persuasive, and the way they have been constructed to produce their effect. Historiographic query must articulate and judge the implicit statesmanship of a history and the implicit judgments about the human condition which it reflects or unstatedly sustains.

While a historian may be working mainly in one or
two modes, he will also presuppose what Buchler calls
"a tangled cluster of doings, makings...assertings" (CM
p. 117). The cluster as a whole has had an effect upon,
and has a cognitive value for, the historian embarking
on his history. If what the historian wishes to do with
his history is add to our knowledge, he will draw upon
the given cluster as a "cognitive fund" for his
cognitive purpose. But if he wishes, say, to tell a
cautionary tale rather, he may draw on this cluster for
dramatizable material and not for a deliberately
cognitive end. Implicitly, however, any good history
effects some cognitive gain. While the artist
interrogates primarily through contriving rather than
through formulating, the historian seeks to verbalize
effectively (exhibitively as well as assertively) the
phenomena he has contrived to uncover, reorder or
reinterpret. For the phenomena he has uncovered or is
reinterpreting, the historian must also devise an
appropriate structure of presentation.

97

Human Action and History

Now the subject of rationality in history, understood as the study of reasons for human actions, is a different subject from that of the rationality of researched and constructed histories. We will take up first the former kind of rationality. This rationality consists, for Buchler, of more than the reasons which can be given assertively for past human actions.

The problem for the philosophic historiographer is that, contrary to most of the Western tradition after Aristotle, rationality is not only an "intellectual virtue" (as in the quotation at the opening of this chapter). If, as Buchler correctly says, "reason is love of inventive communication" (TGT p. 168) and "devotion to query," then rationality can also be a property of practice and an attribute of ingenious contrivance. As B. Singer says in her book on Buchler (ONIJB 1983), if the life of reason is to be a way of living rather than only a way of thinking, it is not enough just to reason assertively about our conduct. We must be able to act in a way that is rational in operation. It follows that the political historian will be described by the historiographer as looking for the rationality _in_ agents' actions and policies as well as for the reasons given in the documents _for_ their actions and policies. And this is indeed what good historians do.

It also follows that the cultural (literary, musical, artistic, scientific, institutional) historian who has this conception of the rationality of creative works will himself be more rational than the historian hypothesized by Popper. For, this historian imparts significance to events only through his preconceived or selective point of view (PH p. 150). Popper claimed that there is no such thing as the explanation of a historical event; he explicates his dictum that "there is no meaning in history" (OSIE p. 453) as signifying that what histories provide are imputed meanings and interests.

According to Popper, historical interpretations are not the kind of thing that can be verified. Interpretations in history, he says, have the same kind of function as theories do in science.[Popper's concept of science, it has to be remembered, is theoreticist or, at best, technological in the sense of applied theory.] But in the works that Popper said this, he also stated his belief that scientific theories as such are verifiable in the senses that he specified. So, theories in science and interpretations in history are, in this important respect, disanalogous on Popper's own account.

Theories, however, as Kuhn and others have pointed out, are themselves never actually tested. What scientists do in fact test in their special sciences are propositions within their theories. Thus, it is the view of science that admits to the speculative component in scientific theories that can make the comparison without disanalogy, not Popper's. But I say this, not to reduce historical interpretations to scientific theories or to exempt scientific propositions from verification, but to remind the reader that scientific theories, like historical interpretations, can well be underdetermined by the facts. Philosophers and historians have pointed this out at some length (OSIE 1950, SSR 1970, ET 1977, CKG 1972, PR 1980, RRPS 1980, RS 1981).

Just as it does not follow that choice among theories is arbitrary because theories, as such, are not strictly speaking verifiable; so, choice among interpretations in history does not have to be arbitrary. Nor is an interpretation "mainly a point of view" (OSIE p. 167 Popper's emphasis), "whose value lies in its fertility," in its ability "to lead us to find new material" or "to help us rationalize (sic) and unify it" or "throw light upon" the historical materials.

Whatever this last vague metaphor may mean, surely all interpretations claim to throw light on the material. This, and all the other questions that Popper's way of talking about interpretations raises-- such as, what does he mean by "rationalize" (as opposed to account for) or, how does the finding of new material by itself make an interpretation more secure-- are questions which refer to the rationality of history books, not to that of human actions in the past. As such, these questions must be kept separate; but they cannot, in any case, be dealt with adequately unless we keep in mind the implications of the fact that all discourse is interpretive, not just the discourse of history. Nor can we allow that that is an "interpretation" which only imparts meaning to actions ad hoc or which is only the rationalization of them from a point of view external to them and their temporal context.

"Saying, doing, and making are equal as forces of history," we read in _Nature_ _and_ _Judgment_; they are equally judicative or effective in the present. Just as an observer is not limited to imputing motives to the actions of another, and is not limited to offering for the present actions of another a rationale which derives _only_ from his own point of view, so the historian of past actions can do better than Popper believes.

The observer who takes note of the determinacies introduced into a situation by an action, is treating the action as a kind of unverbalized choice. He treats it as precluding some possibilities and as leading to others. He has treated it as what Buchler calls an active judgment. The greater difficulty of doing this with actions that now exist only in the records, is only a matter of degree. It does not constitute an impossibility. And just as observers and participants get understanding of current actions and situations by looking at them in the light of the agents' characters and values, their temporal and behavioral antecedents, their institutional involvements, so historians can take an agent-oriented or participant-oriented point of view of past behavior that is itself behavioral and not externalistic. They can, that is, stick to the determinacies introduced by the recovered or recorded actions into situations that were developing in the past which is being studied.

In fact, the more a historian takes past behaviors as active judgments, the less does he run the risk of ascribing anachronistic (merely imputed) rationales to past actions and policies. And if it is past human production in the arts and sciences that the historian must account for, his interpretations will not merely be in terms of the sociohistorical context. They will have to be--in the case of art-works--in terms of both their perceptible, internal aesthetic design and of the effects they have upon their culture and the difference they made to the technical tradition from which they arose.

Externalist interpretations here will express only the would-be historian's preconceptions and preferences. But an internally generated critque that articulates a work's effectiveness in terms of its design and its locus in the communicative situation of its culture, is an interpretation which revalidates the work for the reader as a complex exhibitive judgment. And it is a dealing with products and individuals in terms of their historicity.

We see again that some positivist historiographies are oblivious to the inherently historical and communicative nature of the subject-matter of the human sciences. It can only be because the latter is assimilated to the subject-matter of the natural sciences that it is forgotten that "community and history are ingredients of the self" as Buchler says in TGT (p. 38). What Buchler says about the communicative situation applies to historical discourse (TGT p. 37):

> "when we say that individuals are the relata of communication we must mean individual histories, and, more to the point, individual histories cumulatively represented. In addition, we must imply the presence in the individual of communal traditions--communities cumulatively reflected."

What makes "social experience" possible such that its "lessons" can be appealed to by historians and politicians, or dramatized by journalists and film-makers are the real similarities which "obtain between spans of individual history and spans of other individual histories" (NJ p. 129).

> "Similarity of this kind is proceptive parallelism. Proceptive parallelism makes social history...possible. For without it, the `history' of a group is a history of unrelated masses rather than of representative traits."

Buchler's account of the analysis of historical events in terms of complexes of individual actions, thus avoids the dangers of atomism and reductionism.

> "Proceptive parallelism, instead of implying the reduction of social existence to individual experience, on the contrary prevents the atomization of the social. What we generically call `human experience' is not the mere multiplicity of all human happenings: that is not what we could be urged to `consult'. It is rather the tissue of likeness in individual human histories. We are urged to `appeal' to what can be appropriated in some mode of judgment by one individual and another and still another. It would make no sense to appeal to what is available in one way to this individual, in another to that, and in no way to all" (NJ p. 129)

101

As for the inadequacy of construing the rationality of past human actions and products in terms which are only assertive, Buchler, as we are seeing, has been the first among philosophers to try systematically to supply the inadequacy with fullness and categorial accuracy.

In the history of human affairs at large, including political history, agents do not always confront problem-situations. It is true that, in writing history of science or history of philosophy, the intellectual historian does well to identify the problems to which scientists and thinkers were responding, so that his account of their work or systems as solutions to living problems reflects the concerns of their time. But not all scientific work or all philosophy is inquiry in the sense of problem-solving. Darwin's record of his voyages on The Beagle, and Plato's dialogues are examples which spring to mind here. And since poetry, painting, composing etc. are also not cases of problem solving (except in some incidental respects), the intellectual historian needs to have a conception of rationality wider and deeper than that which assimilates these kinds of intellectual process (Aristotle called it "dianoia") to problem solving.

Interpretive hypotheses in historical query are superseded or replaced because (i) the connections and grounds they offer or (ii) the terms in which they seek to make sense of past events are judged unsatisfactory in relation to all the kinds of evidence available. Since neither active nor exhibitive rationality are nomological, the terms in which the cultural or political historian gives his account will not be subject to the kind of falsification envisaged by the hypothetico-deductive method. To appreciate Buchler's understanding of how interpretations come to be validated, we must complete our sketch of his view of reason and validation. For, an interpretation _is_ the articulation of the rationality or irrationality of past actions and policies, outcomes and assertions. As the questions which the interpretation addresses are legitimated by the interpretation, so the judgment _of_ the interpetation by readers of the history it constitutes will be a judgment about how intelligibly, interestingly or convincingly the history has presented and accounted for the successes and failures of past actions and policies, past products and assertions.

Buchler's Conception of Rationality

> "Rationality could be defined as the willingness to discover other perspectives, to attain community of perspective, and to reconcile community with conviction,"

says Buchler in TGT (p. 116). If the business of the pluralist (or dialectician) and of the intellectual historian is to engage or understand others in terms of _their_ most basic premises, then the above words have described almost the whole endeavor of the philosophic historian.

Before or beyond what was believed, however, the general historian has also to discover "what actually happened," as von Ranke put it. But in human affairs what actually happened cannot be accurately described without an understanding of the beliefs and motivations of the historical actors, and the perspectives--conflicting or overlapping--within which they were interacting. "Man is," for Buchler, "potentially a rational animal--invariably a `symbolical animal' (Cassirer) and perhaps even...a `metaphysical' animal (Schopenhauer)" (NJ p. 153). More fundamentally, "since reason and symbolic activity are most intelligible in terms of the processes of proception and production," man is (for Buchler) the proceiving and judging animal, namely, the agent or reagent, locatable in various orders, who is simultaneously an assimilator and manipulator interacting in a world of potential meanings with other natural complexes or bearers of perspectives.

Thus, it is a premature counself of "epistemological despair," as Dewey and Bentley called it (KK 1949, p. 311), to say that "because social science phenomena are all inextricably bound up with action and because what is peculiar to human action is not capturable by the kind of net employed by natural science....social theory...cannot tell us what the nature of [the social] world is. Social inquiry cannot reveal what human nature is" (Simon UHA 1982, p. 207).

These are negative conclusions forced upon the writer quoted by (i) his narrow assumption that "social science deserves recognition as a...set of cognitive disciplines, only if it is able to represent the elements of human social life as objects, as predictable, and as susceptible to arrangement in systematic order" (UHA p. 169). This writer is also betrayed by (ii) his unexamined assimilation of all reflection to "theory" and all interrogation to "inquiry," as well as by (iii) the generally defective terminology of a tradition that resists all suggestions that there are other modes of knowledge than the theoretical (as Aristotle pointed out) or the assertive (as Buchler has shown). Note also (iv) the illicit process by which Simon infers that if "natural science" can't grasp the peculiarly human, then neither can "social theory" grasp what the social is.

What Buchler points out that Aristotle did not, is that there are other kinds of judgment than Aristotle's practical knowledge (knowledge of practice that issues in right conduct) and productive knowledge (knowledge of making that issues in well-made products). There is also the active judgment which a practice or bit of conduct _enacts_, and there is the exhibitive judgment effected or laid down by the shaped product. It is the viability of this set of distinctions that helps us to see how the historian, as a human scientist, can articulate the meaning or rationality of past actions and constructions while making judgments, explicit or implicit, about the appropriateness of the former or effectiveness of the latter. Buchler's distinctions let us see that it is _because_ the historian deals in interpretations rather than universalizable theories, that he can do his job--not _in spite of_ his failure to invoke the kind of universal laws required by nomotheticists or scientistic theorists.

Speaking of reason, towards the end of TGT, as a "basic candor," as self-reflective as well as scientific, as inventive, expressive and active, Buchler defines superstition, one of the opposites of reason, as "fear of invention--of communication lest it harbor products that demand query." The hastiness, indeed, with which some social science theorists dismiss the possible rationality of expression, invention and action is dangerously akin to the fear of further query pointed to by Buchler: "Those who...are concerned exclusively to affirm principles at the expense of query, are the most insecure of men" (TGT p. 142).

Incompletion must not be cured, however, at the cost of blocking query (TGT p. 169):

"The rational man is willing to undertake the work of interrogation, since he implicitly perceives that the incompletion within life is perpetual and that the denial of query is stagnation and ruin. Reason cannot be a worship of the new; every moment bears newness, and mere persistence...is no rational value. The problem of reason is to discriminate among the potentialities of the new....In the nature of the case there can be no formula for either the achievement or the reward of rationality."

Examples of query in the active mode--e.g. the practice of a rite, a political demonstration, a practice of looking both ways--are easily provided by the reader himself. And Buchler's point should now be clear that the rationality _of_ human actions consists of more than the statable reasons _for_ them, and that this rationality is what historical interpretations also articulate and judge in both the exhibitive and assertive modes. The question which arises next is that of Buchler's conception of the nature of interpretation and of how historical interpretations are validated.

Interpretation, Validation and Works of History

Many of the deeds and utterances produced during the human past, like some purely political "statements," were actually not designed to advance reciprocal, or real, communication. They were calculated rather to achieve an assymetric kind of control or domination. Such utterances do not escape the need for methodic justification by the historian, both in terms of the commitments they reflect, create or disturb and in the sense of having been effected in ambiguous or bimodal ways. That deeds and utterances have historical and communicative effects generates the duty to monitor the way they function. It confirms the aptness of Buchler's characterization of them as judgments, namely, as determinative of ramified consequences.

"Statements" above is put in quotes because in politics what the naive take to be statements are really political _acts_ aimed at creating certain conditions or achieving some hoped-for effects. The active or exhibitive nature of such judgments overrides on analysis the apparently assertive form in which they are couched.

Thus, for example, in Thucydides' history of the Peloponnesian war, when Pericles tells the Athenian Assembly (II.63) that "to recede is no longer possible," this is not truly a statement; nor is it a true statement, since there was no irresistible necessity for Athens to continue expanding its empire as such. It is rather an indirect way of announcing a decision that may not be questioned, namely, that Athens will persist in its method of "defense" by aggressive expansion of its empire. The utterance has a complex referent distinct from its apparent reference, and is not only not true but also not simple. In so far as it includes a claim it is only plausible in combination with other unstated but accepted claims about empire and how to lead or unify the Greek world.

Again, when Brasidas tells the Acanthians at IV.85 that "we Spartans thought of you as allies eager to accept us," he is really telling them he wants them on his side "or else." When he adds "my aim in coming is not...to obtain your alliance but to...help you against the Athenians" (IV.86), he is negating what he just desiderated (i.e. the alliance) and assuming the acceptability of the "help" he is forcing them to accept. Brasidas's "statements," then, are overwhelmingly part of the active judgment constituted by the maneuver of occupying the city of Acanthia. As assertions they are false and contradictory. Functionally, they are verbal phases of an active judgment received as such by the people involved.

Now, we take it with Buchler (and Aristotle) that "physics, history and poetry are cognitive in different respects, not in different degrees" (ML p. 149). So, we see that a good history is like poetry in Buchler's conception: "in so far as it communicates... [it] inculcates an impetus to query of whatever mode, stimulating articulation or utilizations of the [historical] product." In contrast to a good history of politics, however, a tendentiously political history will not only have to be taken as a complex of merely active or exhibitive judgments; it may also succeed in an unstated aim of blocking query.

In the latter case, and where freedom of inquiry exists, the work will fail to be validated as history by responsible historians. It will be recognized for the mainly political act that it is. Here we see one kind of criterion at work among historians: arbitrary interpretations imposed upon the past by requirements external to those of the discipline of history, are dismissed as unhistorical by good historians. This does not mean that good histories do not have an active and an exhibitive dimension, as well as an assertive one. It means, rather, that there have always been criteria for validating historical work in its active and exhibitive dimensions even though the criteria have most often remained implicit.

Another technique of validation would consist in detecting or focussing on the insecurity in a historian's facts or ideas, in order to attain greater security about them (TGT p. 142). Take, for example, the way in which Hexter, in his chapter on Il Principe and lo stato, relates misinterpretations of Machiavelli to the reader's failure to notice the non-systematic and plurivalent way in which Machiavelli uses key terms (VPER 1973, p.150-178), and the reader's failure to pinpoint what invariance there is in the function and connotations of these terms. If, as we may assume, Machiavelli knew very well what he was talking about in The Prince (namely, the modes of predatory politics in contrast to the implicit republicanist standards not made explicit till the Discourses), while the interpretations vary in strange ways among themselves, then any new interpretation that is not to blame Machiavelli for the problem must secure itself not only by relating particular interpretations to the preconceptions of particular interpreters but also by relating the weaknesses in previous interpretations to the texts themselves of Machiavelli.

And it must do so in a way that can withstand the closest scrutiny. Difficulties in the writings themselves, as political reflection or as history, can then be confronted in terms of their coherence and applicability and as themselves part of Machiavelli's interpretations of contemporary politics or Roman and Florentine history. Machiavelli's interpretations of Roman history in the Discourses are developed as derivations of political theory from the republican point of view and are, therefore, to be articulated and criticized as such. They should not be validated or invalidated as expositions or reconstructions of Livy or of the history of the Roman republic. Many readers of Machiavelli have not been sure of what he meant as a historian, and more readers have been too sure of what he represents in the history of political theory because they have been unhistorical in their interpretation of the political reflections and because they have overlooked the republican bias which is present in both the Discourses and The Prince, but is more visible in the former than in the separate, isolated reading which the latter usually receives. We see that seizing upon the conflicts among and insecurities in all the readings of The Prince performed in abstraction from the Discourses and its temporal context, can lead to a better way of reading it and a better interpretation. [This is attempted in my "On the Unity of Machiavelli's The Prince with the Discourses."]

As in other cases of conflicting interpretations, one cannot say that the question of how to read Machiavelli has been definitively resolved. It is rather a matter of validating one reading as better than other inferior readings. But ratification of the new reading does include a feeling of consummation; for, in so far as a historical interpretation is underdetermined by the evidence, it is as an exhibitive and active judgment that it commends itself for approval. As far as the evidence goes, of course, and in so far as the historian has utilized the hypothetico-deductive method (as archaeology or economics, say) this phase of his work remains subject to assertive query--extrapolative as the hypotheses may sometimes have to be in history.

108

But, as noted earlier, once the inferred material has been given body in a historical account it becomes subject, as an account, to the processes of exhibitive and active query. And we have already said that the rationality of past actions and policies themselves is subject to query in all three modes.

The kind of validation that complements assertive query also bypasses the alternatives of acceptance and rejection in the narrow sense of these two terms (TGT p. 157). The test here is the degree to which the exhibitive aspects of the work in fact get assimilated by the public, not the degree to which the work is given explicit critical approval.

"The stronger the product, the greater the opportunity for qualitative assimilation. The greater the impact of an exhibitive judgment on the critical sensibility of its social audience, the greater the degree of its validation."

Regardless of explicit social approval,

"the validity of a work of art [for example] lies in the extent to which it modifies human query; its longevity and repute are significant only in so far as they mirror the depth of the modification."

Let us invoke examples of historical works or theses that "test," illustrate or bring out the limits of this proposal in our context. Bartolome de las Casas's _Brevisima_ _Relacion_ de _la_ _Destruccion_ de _las_ _Indias_ (Engl. tr. 1583), certainly, was both accepted and rejected in different circles in too hasty a way to get discursive articulation. It was immediately applied or misapplied for political purposes. In either case this brief opus deeply affected all subsequent work on the history of Spain and its empire in America.

Gibbon's use of the literary sources in his _De-_ _cline_ _and_ _Fall_ _of_ _the_ _Roman_ _Empire_ (1776-1782) was enormously successful in the respect that it was a major factor in the dramatic flow and vividness of his narrative. But in the respect that it was uncritical of these same sources because source-criticism had not yet been invented, its success set the pattern, insufficiently noted, whereby intellectual historians of Greek antiquity prefer to use whatever secondary sources are extant--no matter how bad they are as evidence--rather than not use them, or use them with the careful skepticism and consistency that historiography requires. For, such skepticism and consistency would force a radical revision of the <u>Hellenistic</u> tradition about Classical thought (c. 480-c. 350 B.C.) which it, circularly, corroborates by being constitutive of it. In resonance with centuries of neoplatonist thought, this kind of bondage to literary "sources" still blocks query about, and unmediated articulation of, the Greek texts of a Plato or a Herakleitos in terms of their own nature, culture or assumptions. The exhibitive nature of Plato's dialogues is shut out, while the poetic nature of Herakleitos's rhythmic and imagistic utterance is subordinated to an anachronistic cosmological interest. And the query that Plato and Herakleitos woud as originals otherwise engender is converted, by the interposition of "the tradition," into a continuing articulation of recognizably pythagorean and idealist questions and assumptions. [This topic is given fuller treatment in my <u>Plato's</u> <u>Dialogues</u> <u>One</u> <u>by</u> <u>One</u> (N.Y. Irvington 1983) and in <u>Rereading</u> <u>the</u> <u>Earlier</u> <u>Presocratics</u>].

The history of the United States has never been the same, so to say, since Beard's <u>An</u> <u>Economic</u> <u>Inter-</u><u>pretation</u> <u>of</u> <u>the</u> <u>Constitution</u> <u>of</u> <u>the</u> <u>United</u> <u>States</u> (1913). Nor can the reading of "Homer" remain unaffected by Milman Parry's historical thesis about the oral-aural nature of the transmission and recomposition of the Homeric epic (1928; 1928). Geoffrey of Monmouth's <u>History</u> <u>of</u> <u>the</u> <u>Kings</u> <u>of</u> <u>Britain</u> (XII century; tr. by St. Evans 1903) could be seen as a challenge to our rule, if its validity as history had not long since been reduced to zero and its influence seen to be that of fiction, ideology and rhetorically well-handled fantasy. Taken in its exhibitive dimension, Hempel's "The Function of General Laws in History" (1942) is now visible as an exploratory <u>act</u> of anti-history couched in theoreticist assertions purporting to be about the practice of history. But it did, for a time, redirect philosophic query about history into channels whose rewards have emerged as very limited.

If the contemporary renewal of interest in the history of science was in some way stimulated by the ensuing reflection about history and explanation, then this must be counted as a positive byproduct of the attempt to impose or assimilate a thesis about history which the practice of history makes it impossible to digest. In the field of the history of science itself, T. Kuhn's essay on the intellectual history of modern science <u>The</u> <u>Structure</u> <u>of</u> <u>Scientific</u> <u>Revolutions</u> (1962), can be said to have significantly modified query in the broad fields where it is being assimilated and appraised.

In illustrating another kind of validation accorded to works on history by the history of their reception in the culture, the above examples also clarify--as history--ways in which interpretations are established or superseded according to non-hypothetico-deductive patterns.

Faced with the finished product, criticism of an exhibitive work must take its start from the working premises of the creator in so far as they can be gathered from his work[s] and the project they imply. This is why even the assent of a maker to a critic's interpretation does not validate it with any finality: to the degree that his project as a creator is developing or taking new directions, the effects of nature and culture upon him and his assumptions will not be clear to him except through their expression in his _oeuvre_. Just as Buchler says "it would be good... if we could assimilate the products of exhibitive query with a creative indecision" (TGT p. 156), so the validation of the work must wait upon the emergence of its relations to other products. Only so, in any case, will its unique contribution be properly appreciated. It is especially clear in works of history that it is in the process of shaping his construction that the historian does much of the historical, "colligational" as opposed to "nomological," validation of his own findings, hypotheses and interpretations.

After all, the history he has composed is the historian's judgment of the complex situations to which he has brought order. So it can be quite arbitrary when a critic brings preformed or external standards to bear on the exhibitive or active dimensions of the historian's work. Only the assertive judgments of the historian permit a repeated reenactment of the verifying conditions; for, as we know, only in assertive judgment are the circumstantial or unique traits of the utterance inessential or irrelevant to its validity. In a history the assertive judgments are made to fit with, or are reinforced and contextualized by, the shape and perspectives of the history. So it is about these internal relations of the work that the critic will have something to say. But since the historian is aware of the relation of his work to other work in the field, he has also helped determine the nature of that rela-

tion. Here, the critic will also be concerned to articulate and judge this set of external relations.

The historian's methods will vary with his aims
both in the development of the evidential material and
the construction of his presentation. But the choice of
method is itself a subject of query. So the historian's
methods which in the first instance are validated by
the coherence, credibility and applicability of his
construction, must in the second instance be articulated and queried by the critical reader of his history.

Different histories of the same events or epoch,
when they draw on different special sciences or use
different practical or prudential principles of interpretation, will provide different kinds of information
about these events or this epoch. Information generated
by different special sciences illuminates different
aspects of agents' actions or of the social process in
a given epoch. A differing sense of what is politically
advantageous, or of what is nation-preserving, or of
what is in the best interest of humanity produces a
different ordering or selection of antecedents for
given events and a different focus upon them.

We see that it is the historians' use of given
special sciences that gives rise to different explanations · of the same events or epoch, but that it is his
power of historical presentation that creates the interpretation of the events or epoch. Explanations, in
the nomological sense, will be continuous with the
historical interpretation within which they are offered. But the historical interpretation as a whole
should not be confused with the special science explanations of actions and events which it facilitates and
incorporates. The interpretation as a whole may feel
like it has explained some events or an epoch; but it
is not an explanation in the nomological sense. Histories as a whole have never had the nomothetic-deductive form required to make them explanations in this
sense. If they did have this form, they would be exercises in historical sociology or historical climatology
etc. rather than social history. The discipline of
history would then be only a special science, not the
architectonic art-and-science it has always been--
including from before the time that the special sciences got invented as separate inquiries. But the selectivity practiced and the reconstructing done by the
history is mainly a matter of judgment in the exhibitive mode, except where there are orientation statements

in the assertive mode or where the historian tries to make his procedure and principles of selection explicit.

A basic historiographic point remains to be made before we illustrate or test and qualify all this by reference to examples. This is that the significance of histories does not come just from their presentation of facts, but from the process whereby the presentation is also an exhibition of a set of factors or determinants. These are those which the historian believes have influenced the course of events. The historian's selection of sociopolitical, ecological etc. antecedents responds to his effort to make intelligible the events of which they are the antecedents in the perspective of human practices. It is in the orders of human practice, of agriculture, of group interaction etc. that the factors (sociological, ecological, political etc.), the selected antecedents, are seen to be efficacious or at least partly determinative of effects.

The historian is not claiming in his work that these factors are causes in the order of physics. Yet, when they are called "causes," as they often carelessly are, they get taken as physical causes--which, of course, they are not. If they are causes (aitiai) in some sense, they are only _historical_ causes: they are the relevant antecedents, in the overlapping orders of politics, geography, technology etc. whose interdependence and ramifications are deployed by the historian in his historical account. These antecedents are seen, by historian and reader alike, as historical causes because they allow us to judge _the effectiveness of the actions_ taken by agents in the history, not because they cause these actions as physical effects.

How _Thucydides_ History _Produces Historical Understanding_

Let us take Thucydides again as our example. Like
other historians, he makes some pointed statements
about some of the methods he has used to gather information and present it. These statements, however, do not
suffice to cover the way he has processed this information or all of what he has actually done in presenting
it.

Thucydides has reminded us at I.xxi that traditional accounts are not reliable (apistōs) because they
are untestable (anekselegta) and because most of them
have won their way (eknenikēkota) to the level of the
mythical (epi to mythōdes). He then tells us (I.xxii)
that the war-related speeches to follow have been reconstructed on the basis of what he and his informants
have been able to recall of what they heard, but (i)
with a care to reproduce for a given speaker on a given
subject the kind of language he could be expected to
have used, and (ii) with a care to stick as closely as
possible to the true overall sense of what was actually
said.

As to the facts of what happened (ta d'ergon tōn
practhentōn) during the war, Thucydides feels that they
deserved systematic (ouk ek tou paratychontos pynthano-
menos) and non-subjective (oud'ōs emoi edokei) attention, even though he had witnessed some of the events
himself. And the reports received about events from
other eye-witnesses were also, he says, minutely gone
through and laboriously balanced. Thucydides hopes his
avoidance of the myth-like (mythōdes) in his recital
(akroasin) will produce a clear view both of the events
which happened in the past and of those in the future
which will recur in accordance with what is human (kata
to anthrōpinon) in such affairs. For him it will suffice, Thucydides says, if those whom his work has
helped in this way judge it to be a permanent acquisi-
tion (ktēma...es aiei).

But this does not tell us why Thucydides needed to
reconstruct whole debates as well as single speeches.
Of the twenty-six or twenty-seven reconstructed speeches, nineteen of them are the parts of eight debates.
The successful speeches, as we know, bring into exhibition the reasons which prevailed for the policies and
actions adopted. The losing speeches, as M. Cogan (THT
1981) has pointed out, complement these by defining--

exhibitively--the political situation and context of events, thus supplying dramatically (by mimēsis) what the narrative has to provide (by telling) in the case of single speeches or indirect discourse.

But the visible design of the history shows that the original reason for reconstructing speeches in the first person at all, is that their presence signals to the reader either that events are at an important turning-point or that new policies or kinds of action are being inaugurated. Where most histories embalm the point of view of the winners, the juxtaposition of contrasting first-person arguments not only restores to parity the views of the losers. It provides an implicit judgment of both winners and losers, of destroyers and destroyed. And human destructiveness receives a fuller criticism in this implicit way than it could in the assertive mode. Thus, Thucydides' device of featuring speeches and debates has permitted him to convey economically, in the exhibitive mode, judgments about the relative importance of actions, policies and phases of the war as well as unstated judgments of value about human agents and events.

What the substantive issues in all their particularity were at the time is made manifest by the dramatizing device of presenting them in a first-person confrontational format. Thucydides' way, here, makes the issues more sharply experienceable than could the reporting of what they were. But in the famous dialogue (V.lxxxv-cxiii) between the Melians and the Athenians (an exchange consisting of twenty-seven parts) it is the Sophistic _manner_ of winning arguments by presupposing coercive force to be on the Sophists' side that is also highlighted.

The Athenians have come, in full force, to make the island-city of Melos a subject of their empire. But the Melians are, tribally, kin to the Spartans and would prefer to remain neutral in the war. The Athenians propose a procedure for discussing their differences which will avoid mere speechmaking and consist of a point by point exchange, interruptible at any time, and without hindrance of any audience other than the negotiators (V.lxxxv).

The Melians agree to the procedure, but take exception to the overwhelming force brought by the Athenians which makes them "judges in their own cause." Here the implicit repugnance of the Sophistic habit of going into any discussion with a pre-established conclusion (rather than an open mind), and of giving arguments for it (rather than looking for what the communicative interaction might yield), is put into stark exhibition. And it is made to resonate with the (ordinarily unnoticed) inhumanity of the other Sophistic practice of always taking the position that puts force on their side. The Melians also recognize that the Athenians are offering a false alternative, annihilation or slavery to the empire. It is an inescapable alternative because of the force behind it, not because it is exhaustive as true alternatives should be (V.lxxxvi).

The Athenians respond that if the Melians fail to consult anything but their safety (i.e. expediency), the debate will be terminated. So, at lxxxix, the Athenians start again with the standard false-pretense-to-honesty which is but another Sophistic mask for siding with dominant force. Right, they claim, can only be discussed between equals in power. So the Melians urge upon the Athenians the practical consequence that not to be able to invoke justice deprives all states of a refuge in principle that the Athenians may one day need. The Athenians spurn this.

From xci on communicative distortions break out like a rash in the discourse of the Athenians, as a result of the kind of power politics--polarizing expansionism--that they are practicing. "Preservation" is offered as a code-word for "subjection." The "good" the Melians are offered is only good for the Athenians, and actually only a lesser evil than annihilation for the Melians. "Tolerance" becomes "weakness" for the empire (xciv), and the neutrality of any islanders is a dangerous "threat" to the masters of the sea (xcvii-xcix). The reader is at one and the same time being shown--without need of analytic comment--both what is destructive about Sophistic rhetoric and its cynical presupposition, and how the Sophistic formulation of an Athenian policy leads to the destructiveness consequent upon radical polarization. We also see, from Thucydides' design, that he is in good control of the exhibitive dimension of his work, even though the text as we have it looks like an incompletely revised draft. Thucydides' exhibitive strategies offset a density of narrative detail that might otherwise have dampened the history's effectiveness.

Of course, not all historians are so much in control of the exhibitive aspect of their work, as we saw in the example of Gibbon's uncritical use of literary sources, or as can be seen in the pro-Spartan Hellenica of Thucydides' mediocre continuator Xenophon. But the negative cases, it can safely be said, only confirm our rule that one most basic cause of the effectiveness of a historical work is what is called its design or rhetorical organization, but is also its exhibitive dimension. [The latter term is the more adequate one in implying that the design itself implements a judgment in a non-assertive mode, and because what we call the design of a work may not exhaust its exhibitiveness.]

The reference here is to the critic's appraisal of a work as history, not to his analysis of it as suggesting social science explanations but to the critic's assessment of the work as an ordering of events, actions and facts in a usable historical way. For, there is (as we have said), a definable difference between judging a work as historical sociology or ecology etc. and judging it as history, just as there is between the art criticism or literary criticism of works from the past and a history of art or history of literature.

What Thucydides sees as historical "causes" of events and decisions are, observably, either precipitating circumstances which were the starting points of action or reasoning (aitiai, archai), or else they are general individual attitudes or dispositions such as the sense of Athenian power or of collective skill in seamanship etc. As turning points, events of the first sort are also points of reference in the narrative. As decisions or things done they are, naturally, not always self-determined but are determined in other ways and by other events and actions. Clearly, the historian's citation of "the" determining antecedents of an action or outcome does not exhaust, or attempt to exhaust, the causal determinacy of the event in the physicalist or special-science sense of "cause" or "determined."

But it does seem to make the event intelligible in the order of historical discourse. The rehearsal of the relevant antecedents does this by locating the events to be understood (as history) in a perspective of practical statesmanship. As the superlative historian that he is, Thucydides also succeeds, like a Greek drama, in locating the events of his history in what I call a perspective of humanity. Thus for example, the reader comes to feel that, had the Athenians heeded

117

Pericles' prudent verbal advice to their Assembly (I.144) "not to combine schemes of new conquest with the conduct of the war" and abstain from risky involvements, they could have avoided their huge losses in Sicily and their final tragic defeat. But the reader has also been primed by the author to see that Pericles' speech is partly self-contradictory and partly in contradiction with actual policy. He has been allowed to see further that, in their responses to the circumstances and temptations of power, the Athenians were misled into exceeding--in their actions--the limits of wise practice by self-serving and Sophistic habits of reasoning and speaking about the circumstances.

Bibliography

HPW Vc. B.C. Thucydides _History of the Peloponnesian War_ 4 vols. text & tr. C. Forster (Loeb Libr. 1919-1928)

XH IVc. B.C. Xenophon _Hellenica_ text & tr. C.L. Brownson (Loeb Libr. 1918-21)

HKB XIIc.A.D. Geoffrey of Monmouth _History of the Kings of Britain_ tr. S. Evans (Everyman reprint)

TPAD 1516- N. Machiavelli _The Prince and the Discourses_ ed. M. Lerner (Modern Library 1940)
     1522

BRDI 1552- B. de las Casas _Brevisima Relacion de la Destruccion de las Indias_ English tr. (London: Brome 1583)
     1583

DFRE 1776- E. Gibbon _Decline and Fall of the Roman Empire_ 3 vols. ed. J.B. Bury (N.Y. Heritage Press repr. 1946)
     1782

EIC 1913 C. Beard _An Economic Interpretation of the Constitution_ (N.Y. Macmillan; new Intro. 1935)

LSD 1935 K. Popper _Logik der Forschung; The Logic of Scientific Discovery_ (N.Y. Basic Books 1959)

LTI 1938 J. Dewey _Logic: The Theory of Inquiry_ (N.Y. Holt)

FGLH 1942 C. Hempel "The Function of General Laws in History," _The Journ. of Philosophy_, vol.39

KK 1949 J. Dewey & A. Bentley _Knowing and the Known_ (Boston: Beacon)

OSIE 1950 K. Popper _The Open Society and Its Enemies_ (Princeton: 1950 1 vol. ed.)

TGT 1941 J. Buchler _Toward a General Theory of Human Judgment_ (N.Y. Columbia; rev. w. new Intro. Dover 1979)

NJ 1955 J. Buchler _Nature and Judgment_ (N.Y. Columbia; repr. Grosset 1966)

PH   1957   K. Popper The Poverty of Historicism (London: Routledge)

CM   1961   J. Buchler The Concept of Method (N.Y. Columbia)

HRT   1967   J. de Romilly Historie et Raison chez Thucydide (Paris: Les Belles Lettres)

MNC   1966   J. Buchler Metaphysics of Natural Complexes (N.Y. Columbia)

PDGS   1969   Adorno, Popper et al. German ed. of The Positivist Dispute in German Sociology Engl. ed. by D. Frisby (N.Y. Harper 1976)

SSR   1970   T. Kuhn The Structure of Scientific Revolutions 2 ed. (Univ. of Chicago)

CGK   1970   I. Lakatos & A. Musgrave Criticism and the Growth of Knowledge (Cambridge U.P.)

SOT   1973   H.H. Harding The Speeches of Thucydides (Oklahoma: Coronado)

SIT   1973   P.A. Stadter The Speeches in Thucydides (Univ. of N. Carolina)

VPER   1973   J.H. Hexter The Vision of Politics on the Eve of the Reformation (N.Y. Basic Books)

ML   1974   J. Buchler The Main of Light (N.Y. Oxford)

DHOT   1975   W.K. Pritchett ed. Dionysius of Halicarnassus on Thucydides (U. of Calif.)

CIT   1975   L. Edmunds Chance and Intelligence in Thucydides (Harvard U.P.)

MSH   1975   P. Skagestad Making Sense of History (Oslo: Universitetsforlaget)

ET   1977   T. Kuhn The Essential Tension (Chicago U.P.)

PR   1980   G. Gutting ed. Paradigms and Revolutions (Notre Dame U.P.)

RRPS   1980   M. Hesse Revolutions and Reconstructions in the History of Science (Notre Dame)

EXT 1980 D. Proctor *The Experience of Thucydides* (Warminster: Aris & Phillips)

STH 1981 H.R. Rawlings *The Structure of Thucydides' History* (Princeton U.P.)

HT 1981 M. Cogan *The Human Thing*. The Speeches and Principles of Thucydides' History (Chicago U.P.)

UHA 1982 M. Simon *Understanding Human Action* (Albany: SUNY Press)

PDOBO 1983 V. Tejera *Plato's Dialogues One by One*. A Structural Interpretation (N.Y. Irvington)

ONIJB 1983 B. Singer *Ordinal Naturalism*. Introduction to the Philosophy of Justus Buchler (Assoc. Univ. Presses)

Chapter VI

The Dimensions of History

History, Ideology and the Pragmatic Criterion

Though general history can produce alienation because, as the history of the "winners," it appears to celebrate domination, intellectual history well performed can produce liberation. This is because it increases the range of our identifications in a non-escapist way, and because it shows us which of our besetting problems are only inherited muddles and which are really central to our time (cf. J.H. Randall, ch. IV). The abuse of history which takes the form of an excessive historicism can also be alienating, as Nietzsche pointed out in The Use and Abuse of History (1873-1876). But there is nothing so disappointing or escapist as a history, general or intellectual, which does not relate to the life of its times in a way that is meaningful to us.

However, it is just when a history has uncovered what the interests were and what the distribution of power was which lay behind the things said, done or believed in a given society, that it can be seen that the historical agents--and the historian himself--are implicated in a doubtful relation to the truth. This is the relationship between what is being claimed overtly and what is actually being done or latently pursued as the goal or interest of the historical agents, or historical writers. At this point some students of ideology step in to say that once the historian of ideology has shown that social, personal or material interests always underlie (determine) what people say or do, the historian's own criticism of ideology becomes suspect because there must be an underlying interest which determines it.

But is the critique of ideology, implicit or explicit, itself necessarily ideological? Hans Barth the publicist and theorist (TI 1961) thinks it is; but Lewis Feuer the historian of science (IAI 1975) thinks it is not. Barth's argument was that if "the sum...of intellectual creations represents nothing more than the material conditions and power-relations under which organisms flourish" (TI p. 175), then the intellectual who is claiming this to be the case cannot, by his own reasoning, be objective either.

While it can be granted that all ideas arise from some interest, some sets of ideas are not the unrevised or unexamined result of wishfulness or psychosocial conditions. Nor is it impossible for them to achieve objectivity in the corrigible sense to be specified below. Just as a historian can recognize and document examples of false consciousness, he can also recognize sheer invention or fictive construction and distinguish it from reconstructions based on evidence. Consult, as an instance, the work of R. Levillier uncovering the anti-Hispanic malice and tendentious errors of Clements Markham's translation of the Chronicle of Sarmiento de Gamboa, published unwittingly by the Hakluyt Society in 1907 (Don Francisco de Toledo Vol. III 1942).

Historical reconstructions may be just as interpretive as fictions but they are not imposed upon the evidence; rather, they are drawn from it. There will be ways of testing the hypothetical aspects of a historical account, and judgments can be made about its extrapolative or analogical dimensions by reference to the state of our knowledge, the state of our practices and the human order of our priorities. Fictive accounts in history, as in journalism, are likely to make their appeal to unchecked beliefs, customary assumptions or obtrusive priorities less basic than what I call our human priorities.

The order of values represented by the latter phrase is not non-problematic, but it is the most basic that can be appealed to in historical appraisals. And though appealing to it is a matter of art and mostly an implicit process, the surprising thing is that it remains an operative order and a source of norms in the history of civilization. In contrast to it, nationalist preconception, partisan preference, social and intellectual fashions appear, in the end, to be ephemeral and unsatisfactory bases of judgment. For adherents of ideological accounts it is just the compatibility of the account, and its conclusions, with the dogmas and slogans of the ideology that makes them believable.

"Bias," as Barbara Tuchman says (PH 1981, p. 59), "is only misleading when it is concealed." This has to be said because a historian cannot approach his subject without an interest. At the very least he must be convinced of the significance of his subject and its pertinence. Without this interest he would be without the energy to do it justice or to treat it at all. Now, it appears that a condition of objectivity in history is completeness of information. So the writer who is more interested in a thesis than in a subject will tend to be content with the evidence that seems to corroborate the thesis. He will not be inclined to look for, or he will tend to scant, evidence that might confute or complicate his thesis. The writer armed with an ideological principle will hardly be capable, in his data-gathering, of going beyond evidence that confirms the principle. If the evidence is in conflict with the principle, it may not even be seen as evidence.

Open-mindedness in respect to possible or alternative interpretations is required for the collecting of adequate, more or less complete, information on a given subject. This is because the very interest that makes a historian sensitive to sources of evidence is an abstractive interest. Furthermore, in the assembling of his materials the historian has to be selective in another sense. This is the sense in which he employs principles which organize his materials into a readable account, an account which will of necessity be interpretive. So it is here that either ideology and preconception or, else, real candor and responsiveness to the material will come into operation.

The craftsmanly historian who wants to avoid misunderstanding and to let his account make sense on its own will not hide but will state or signal his interests, his organizing principles and his sympathies. We saw, for example, how few orientation statements Thucydides needed to make, while yet remaining transparent in his sympathies and transparent as to his selectivity. Contemporary historians are wise in preferring to be more explicit about their methods, their principles of selection and the special-science theories they have used in completing particular inquiries or in addressing disputed questions within their particular subjects. But if they wish to remain readable, or to get beyond the raw social science level of presentation, the way they organize their store of materials will both reflect the thoroughness with which they have worked through the evidence and project their interests in an unmasked way.

How in fact is a historian to interest his readers except by sharing or respecting their interests while getting them to share or respect his? Mistaken antipathies and mistaken theories, such as those of the racist history books of the Nineteenth century, may require time to pass before the general public spots them as mistaken. But professional readers should take less time to discount them as historically dubious, as ideological--even while the politicians continue to appeal, in their Sophistic practice, to the prejudices that made the mistakes possible in the first place.

The list of ideological histories that have ceased to serve as histories because of their originally hidden or excessive bias is a long one, and not worth cataloguing except as evidence for later intellectual historians seeking to document attitudinal fashions. On the other hand, the historian who anticipates his readers' skepticism will be sure to make his evidentiary bases more visible and his personal biases more discountable. In fact and as methodic creator, the historian is being true to his medium (historical narrative) when his formative designing supports or modulates the inferential pregnancy, the representational possibilities of the factual and documentary materials with which he is reconstructing a segment of the human past.

Objectivity, as Dewey and other American philosophers have convincingly shown, is not a matter of the "correspondence" between a discourse and some state of affairs in a one-to-one pictorial sense. For the correspondence between the state of affairs and our idea of it to be testable, we would have to have access to the state of affairs independently of our ideas of it; and this is impossible. Nor is the truthfulness of an account to be equated with its certainty. Knowledge begins to be objective when it is shared, when it can be publicly or repeatedly confirmed or disconfirmed.

Thinkers now agree that we should not call a hypothesis true, however certain it may seem, if there is no possible way in which it can be falsified; for, then it would be tautological. This makes truth claims a matter of verifiability. But since verification is only confirmation of the hypothesis by an always insecure "affirmation of the consequent," as logicians call it, confirmation is never final. A hypothesis can be refuted definitively, however, because the "denial of the consequent" by which it is refuted is a logically necessary relation. So, if it is admitted that only claims which are falsifiable qualify as claims that can be empirically true, then it cannot be denied that a trait of good hypotheses is their <u>corrigibility</u>.

If a hypothesis can never be definitively confirmed at the empirical level, it must be such that it does not close off inquiry. And this means that it must be such that it is ever open to improvement or amendment, namely, that it is corrigible. Hence C.S. Peirce's emphasis, in his definition of truth at CP 5.565, on the investigator's need to realize the imperfection of his proposals, and that it is only of approximations to the truth that, after verification (5.569, lines 21f.), we predicate "true" and "false." Peirce's definition of truth at 5.407, on the other hand, invokes the concept of the community of scientific investigators out of whose continuing investigations and experimentally tested agreements and differences the truth comes and continues to be perfected.

In an assertive discourse, then, where the concept of truth applies it is not a matter of denotative or pictorial correspondence with its subject-matter, nor is it anything certain, untestable or unrevisable; nor may the truth close off inquiry. Now, while this applies to the assertive dimension of history, the reader will also have noticed that I am not making the standard appeal from ideology to the scientific method. My reason for this is that historical accounts, as accounts, are not only or mostly a matter of scientific hypotheses. Just as importantly, historical accounts are not theoretical either. Exclusive of the generalizations made by speculative philosophers of history or by speculative anthropologists who intend some reference to human history, practicing historians do not advance a general theory about their subject. When the practicing historians' accounts are analytic as well as narrative, they can more easily be seen to be making a case for a given interpretation of a set of actions or events. But to be making a case, even when it is done with lawyer-like "induction," is not the same as to be theoretical in the nomological sense. So it would be only partly to the point to claim that history the discipline can avoid being ideological by being "scientific," if it is only nomologically scientific in some respects.

Also because histories are interpretive even when functioning in the assertive mode, they tacitly offer only one or two members of an unstated plural alternative--the other members being all the alternative interpretations to which the documents and evidence might give countenance. In logical terms this means that what histories do, in so far as they are assertive, is legitimate the suppression of unstated alternative interpretations by the convincing affirmation of their stated interpretation. This means that good historians, who begin by being open to all the possibilities, always also begin from a tacit multiple alternative. So that, if they had to make an assertion about their subject at this initial stage, they would assert an alternative only, namely, a complex relationship not a complex of facts: "either a1 or a2 or a3...a1 and an or a2 and an." Implicitly, then, historians as such do not assert their interpretations categorically. Tacitly and architectonically they develop and modulate some alternatives among a number of hypothetical interpretations.

A locus classicus for this insight about the logic of the first move which all historians must make, is to be found in Jacob Burckhardt's The Civilization of the Renaissance in Italy:

> "In the wide ocean onto which we venture, the possible ways and directions are many, and the same studies which have served for this work might easily, in other hands, not only receive a quite different treatment and application, but also lead to essentially different conclusions."

[The learned historiographer and photographer S. Kracauer also quotes this passage in his very relevant work History. The Last Things before the Last, 1969]. Good historians, finally, not only make no claims for a general theory; they simply propose, like good artists, fresh angles under which to see the phenomena which they are recovering or reviewing. And it is in the nature of "the historical world," namely, of the materials with which they deal that historians should not want to do more than this.

While histories make an appeal to scientific truth in the assembling of their material, in also constituting communicative interactions with their audiences histories make an appeal to the interest in freedom which is constitutive of the humanity of the society. This implicit appeal is to what Habermas (KHI 1971) calls "the emancipatory interest" in withstanding anti-human or heteronomous domination. This means that, like the works of art which histories resemble in this respect, works of history presuppose not only freedom of inquiry but also undistorted or uncoerced communication.

The Art and Science of History in Classic American Philosophy

Philosophic historiography in N. America is autochthonous because it took its rise from two complex ideas which are distinctive of American thinkers in the English language. One was William James's rich interactional reconception of the notion of "experience." British empiricism had so impoverished the idea as to make it useless for purposes of systematic philosophy, namely, for the purpose of understanding art, science, history or the human process in coordinate and equally adequate terms. The other was C.S. Peirce's idea of the ongoing community of critical and experimental investigators out of whose work and agreement the truth emerges, ever ready to be rectified and retested. While some readers of Peirce are uneasy with the fact that this turns the idea of truth into a limiting conception only, the associated idea itself of the community of investigators was a product of Peirce's close observation of the history and practice of the nomological sciences.

The operant reality of this community has been more and more brought home to philosophers by the work of the historians of science. This reality is important to historiography because without it there would be no way of developing, or judging among historical interpretations. It is among the communities of investigators that we can study the differential way in which historical interpretations are validated, in contrast to the way in which natural science theories or social science hypotheses are.

A generation later John Dewey appropriated something from each of these master notions for purposes of his own transactionist emphasis on "the existential matrix of inquiry," as he was to call it. This emphasis was societal and biological, and not in any sense antihistorical. It was also "naturalist" in a sense not to be confused with either the materialism of the positivists or with what the phenomenologists call "the natural attitude." The addition of Santayana's The Life of Reason (1905-06) to the canon of works attempting to naturalize and socialize our understanding of the human process, made it quite clear that the new movement in N. America was also an imaginative humanism that was in no way either anti-science or anti-humanities. This enlarged, historicized and naturalized, humanism represented by Dewey and Santayana was, however, not blind to the limitations of "science" mechanistically or physicalistically understood. Nor were James, Dewey and Santayana insensitive to or simplistic about mankind's spiritual needs and expressive achievements.

With regard to the discipline of history all the thinkers reviewed in this book have been aware that it is partly a nomologically scientific discipline and partly a literary or humanistic one, namely, that it is an art-and-science or techne in Aritotle's sense. We have developed the nonobvious, yet empirical, senses in which this is the case for these thinkers. We will now focus some more upon what our thinkers have in common and on what the overall outcome for philosophy is of their reflection upon, and practice of, historiography.

That the application of analytic epistemology to historical studies had the effect of downgrading them to bad science, as analytic epistemology understands science, and of entirely neglecting the literary and exhibitive dimensions of history, should have given serious pause to the enthusiasts of that approach. Coupled with the associated failure of Analytic epistemology to deal adequately with the processes of art, the inadequacy becomes a strong signal that there is something misconceived about a philosophy or a method that casts so murky a light upon the distinctively human activities, while claiming to have thrown so much light upon the natural sciences. Either the latter are the only distinctively human activities for the epistemological approach or, else, it has not adequately focussed upon the natural sciences themselves as distinctively human activities.

In contrast, and as a consequence of their broader interpretation of science, the American philosophers reviewed here have all been less one-sided and less scientistic in their characterization of the distinctively human activities. Because reflective thinking about the latter in the West properly begins with Plato and Aristotle, the better understanding of Plato and Aristotle which is to be found in Woodbridge, Santayana, Randall and Buchler must be taken as more than a starting point for them on this subject. Their recovery of the non-Latin Aristotle--the humanist and naturalist--and of the non-systematic Plato--the non-Neoplatonist and dialogical Socratic--has to be seen by the historian as an important constitutive element of their philosophies.

Rightly understood, Aristotle was a pluralist in several senses. The arts-and-sciences, for him, each had their independent premises or starting points which are neither reducible to the assumptions of some all-embracing science nor deductively unifiable. Plato was a pluralist in the sense that, in his dialogues, he used and played with all the doctrines and arguments of his day in order to construct his dramatized intellectual encounters. His imaginary conversations are his exhibitive critique of these doctrines, arguments and other phenomena of his culture. [See my Modes of Greek Thought (1971) and Plato's Dialogues One by One (1983)]. The practical and productive arts-and-sciences, the "technes," are no less knowledges for Aristotle than the theoretical sciences. And he was not only open to more than one kind of knowledge, he was encyclopaedically active in the pursuit of all branches of knowledge.

Now, the insights of pluralism crossfertilize the work of the philosophers under review to the point where Aristotle's pluralism itself could not remain unrevised. It was to receive, as we have seen, an improved formulation in terms of Buchler's principles of ontological parity and the three modes of judgment. Whatever is, or is discriminable, is real. It prevails in some order and is complex. What we call art and action, no less than what we call science, are judicative or judgmental in their own way. The distinctively human activities in Buchler thus receive a more adequate, less theoreticist characterization in terms of the orders within which humans manipulate and assimilate, proceive and judge the subjects they encounter. Dewey's insight that the history of human development is, in practice, traceable as the history of the arts and sciences can be purged of its intellectualist bias. Problem-solving inquiry is no longer the only mode in which the past can be explored or reconstructed. "Inquiry" is replaced by the broader, multi-modal "query," and to the assertive mode of judging and producing are added the active and exhibitive modes. The integrity of past activities and products is better preserved or recovered if the historian or critic can see these activities and products as the kind of determinations which they originally were, and if he is no longer bound to deal only assertively with them.

When Schneider denied that the historical past as a whole has the form of a biography, he was warning that if historians impose the form of a life-cycle or a "career" upon their particular subjects, then their accounts tend to take on the shape of a "rise and fall" that may not suit their subjects and may distort the sequences involved. Nonetheless, the impulse behind Woodbridge's claim that the biographical metaphor is necessary when the subject is groups and behind Randall's view that it is suggestive when the subject is philosophy, is a right impulse. It is an impulse to save the historians's subject, whatever it might be, from being dehumanized by the account that is given of it.

If the account is too abstract, as in some "universal histories" or some monumental histories of art, or if the account reduces its subject to xclusively special-science terms, the result falls short of being good history either because it is too schematic and speculative or because it is "only" special science. On either alternative the human processes involved will have been denatured, detemporalized and emptied of their circumstantiality and intentionality. The self-determination at work in human processes becomes uncharacterizable, and reasons for (as opposed to causes of) actions and decisions become irrelevant. So do norms, implicit or explicit. The human interest, in short, is eliminated by both sorts of history. But the elimination of the implicit human interest from what purports to be a historical account is a sure sign that the account, like ideology, has passed over into pseudo-history.

The vast secondary elaboration of the nomothetic-deductive or natural-science notion of explanation, that unusable byroad ending in the trivialization of the connective tissue of historical discourse, does not appear in the historiography of our thinkers. Our thinkers, rather, are interested in human agency, in the determining and self-determining effects of agents who are themselves social and historical products even if capable of rationality. As for the language of this connective tissue, it is better conceptualized as a phase of the framing-strategies which historians must employ to suggest continuity and parallelism or to assert simultaneity or sequence among events. This language should not be taken as establishing causes in a physicalist or nomothetic-deductive way.

Our eight thinkers avoid the assumption encouraged by logical atomism that there are atomic events or atomic facts. This is the assumption that led such thinkers as Bertrand Russell to believe that connections asserted among events must always be imputed or nominal connections. But this separates "particulars" too sharply from "universals." Because particulars come within a process of selection which is not passive, particulars are not blank or opaque any more than they are atomic. As the result of selection they come steeped in associations and loaded with relations. Correspondingly universals, when not stipulated to be invariable (and, therefore non-existential), are better seen as generalizations ever subject to correction as the ramifications among them thicken or widen or fade, and as new perspectives create new orders or levels in which to locate sets of particular complexes. The process within which new ways of generalizing emerge is of a piece with the process by which particulars change the nature of their complexity or come to look differently. These generalizations become definitional and may be treated as atemporal universals only for deductive (mathematical) purposes. It is a fallacy of material affirmation to take them categorically or as applying to all existence. Because historical accounts--if they are to be historical--cannot proceed deductively or atemporally, they have no need to take corrigible generalizations to be invariant universals.

Nor is the human individual, for our thinkers, an isolated subject needing proof that there is an "external" world out there before he can make contact with it. "Community and history are ingredients of the self," as Buchler says (TGT p. 38). And historical agents are historical not only because they are located in the order of history-in-the-making, but also because their individuality is the resultant of a self-conditioning (Mead, PA p. 108) which supervenes upon the cultural and sociohistorical products which human persons generically are.

History, in short, is a pervasive dimension of human experience and human activity. As such, history is something that the social sciences must either abstract from or come to terms with. It is not so much that the social scientist who is not aware of the way in which he has abstracted from history will not be able to come to terms with the historical dimension of his study, but that he will remain unaware of the limitations of his sociology and of the ground of its inadequacy as a human science. Because history is a human science in senses which should now be clear, we are able to reiterate that as a mixed study historiography will consist of both literary or rhetorical studies and "research-theoretical" studies. [The terms in quotes are mine, however, not those used by our eight thinkers]. But G.H. Mead was explicit in stating his experimentalist view (PA) that the philosophy of science is the theory of research. And this insight of Mead's anticipated a significant new direction now bearing fruit in the philosophy and history of science.

Also of significance for the practice of philosophizing today is the interest in and respect for the discipline of history shown by just the thinkers under review. The lack of fuller treatment of the subject by W. James may be supplied by reference to that of the other founder of Pragmatism, Peirce. While all of Peirce's work reflects his knowledge of the history of natural sciences, Vol. VII of the Collected Papers provides an introduction to the topic. Peirce's view of natural science in its history calls for separate study. The reader should be advised that paragraphs 162-225 collected by the editors under the heading of "Logic of History" do not constitute a historiography. It is, fortunately, quite clear that incomplete as the explicit remarks of these two founders might be they were not lacking in historical consciousness.

More than lacking an interest in history, some "linguistic" philosophers, such as G. Graham (HT 1982, XXI, 1) believe that there can be no such thing as the history of philosophy! Graham does not deny that other kinds of history are possible. But if the histories of both things that change and things that do not change are possible, and if histories of intellectual matters are possible, then so is history of philosophic ideas or systems possible. It has in fact been done. Because some idealist thinkers sometimes confuse historical with philosophical reasoning, Graham overreacts by trying to show, in his own words, that "the `history' of philosophy is just philosophy itself" (p. 48).

Paradoxically, this is the same equivalence that he has been trying to refute within the Analytic tradition, namely, that philosophy is not history of philosophy. Graham has, in other words, maintained both "p" and "not-p". He is also saying something idealistic when he claims that the learning of facts from language is not empirical (p. 49). In any case, this book hopes to have shown that, while a thinker like Randall occasionally confuses the entirety of Western philosophy with the history of philosophy, the practice of the history of philosophy and the practice of philosophy are distinct but mutually enhancing activities. The practice of either one of them singly always tends to the detriment of that practice.

Both Santayana and Mead perceived that epic histories produce effects which rhetorical analysis would call mythological, and that epic histories therefore also risk being ideological in their own way--even when based on ascertained facts. All our thinkers recognize that the quality of a historian's statesmanship will reflect, in some way, the ethos of his own time and culture. But because our thinkers never went into the requisite detail, and because the histories some of them wrote are intellectual histories, one does not find among them a strong enough condemnation of the widespread practice of manufacturing, categorizing and abusing facts for nationalist or other ideological purposes. [In so far as the studies of German thought which Dewey and Santayana wrote during World War I can be said to be historical, they are intellectual critiques of ideology which are themselves not free of ideology (GPP and EGP respectively, 1915).]

In history, as in war, truth is always the first casualty, as Knightly calls it (FC 1975), if the ideological impulse is not controlled. And this is worth noting because it reminds us that the universe of historical discourse is one in which it is felt that justice should prevail, even though the historian is required to record the cases in which justice did not prevail. This characteristic of written history is paralleled by the aesthetic demand made upon it to be coherent and continuous as reading matter, at the same time that it is a record of all kinds of breaks and discontinuities, discordances and contingencies.

It is thus apriorist to believe, as Morris Cohen seemed to believe (MHH 1947, Ch. 4), that historical discourse must, like the natural sciences, conform to the principle of sufficient reason. It was clear already in Dewey (AE p. 85, EN p. 181) that "the logic of animism," namely, non-causal ways of associating events, are common in poetic discourse. So to the extent that the historians' prose obeys poetic principles, its logic will be superpropositional as Dewey called it. And we have seen that, in so far as he is in dialogue with his fellow humans, the historian cannot shed implicit--if problematic--norms of justness and fair dealing.

As explained in Chapter II, narrative accounts
work according to principles different from those of
nomologically scientific discourse. In being artful,
the historian's prose operates to both aesthetic and
ethical effect. The attempt to reduce the lingusitic
tissue connecting the human events presented by a history to nomothetic-deductive form is question-begging.
It leaves out the need for aesthetic analysis of whatever framing strategies historians are in fact using,
by assuming that these will all fit a pre-given form.
This not only blocks query and is unnoticedly sophist-
ical, it assumes that the job of histories is only to
explain in some natural-science sense of explain.

The phenomena of history are always singular in
some way, or circumstantially conditioned in such a way
that it is the apparent repetitions which stand in need
of further analysis. Meanwhile, the norms according to
which their surrounding circumstances are selected as
relevant, are either the norms of practical statesmanship or, else, of the practice of the art or science
whose history is being told. Parallels in history are
never more than parallels in some precarious respects;
and the careful historian, like the man of action,
cannot afford to neglect the respects in which they are
disanalogous.--Witness, for example, the disastrous
consequences of having taken the situation in Vietnam
in the 'Sixties to be analogous to that of Korea in the
early 'Fifties.

That it is wise to remember, with Santayana, that
those who know no history are condemned to repeat it,
does not entail that there are laws of history. Santayana's implication was that men tend to make the same
kinds of mistake in varying circumstances unless fore-
warned. A history focusing on these mistakes would not
show that they had occurred according to some general
law. [If a general law could be proved for them, then
they would not be mistakes]. And if, as is often said,
every generation must be allowed to make some of its
mistakes in its own way, the historian's interest would
then be in the particular way and conditions in which
the mistake was made, or the experience acquired. Such
a history would show that the failures of human agents,
like their successes, are not predictable in the kind
of detail that is the substance of history. As a human
study, the substance of history is in fact a
compounding of circumstantial narrative and more or
less explicit reasoning with implicit ethical

perspectives, all of this within determinate kinds of coherence-creating frameworks.

Bibliography

CRI 1860 J. Burckhardt _The Civilization of the Renaissance in Italy_ (Phaidon repr. 1944; Engl. tr. 1878)

ADHL 1874 F. Nietzsche _On the Advantage and Disadvantage of History for Life_ tr. by P. Preuss of _Vom Nutzen und Nachteil der Historie fuer das Leben_ (Indianapolis: Hackett 1980)

LR 1905– G. Santayana _The Life of Reason_ 5 vols.
1906 (N.Y. Scribner's)

CSG 1907 Clement Markhams "tr." of _The Chronicle of Sarmiento de Gamboa_ (Hakluyt Society 1907)

GPP 1915 J. Dewey _German Philosophy and Politics_ (N.Y. Holt)

EGP 1915 G. Santayana _Egotism in German Philosophy_ (N.Y. Scribner's)

EN 1925 J. Dewey _Experience and Nature_ 1 ed. (Open Court)

AE 1934 J. Dewey _Art as Experience_ (N.Y. Minton Balch)

MHH 1947 M.R. Cohen _The Meaning of Human History_ (Open Court)

TGT 1951 J. Buchler _Toward a General Theory of Human Judgment_ 2 ed. (N.Y. Dover 1979)

CP 1931– C.S. Peirce _Collected Papers_ 8 vols. ed.
1958 Hartshorne, Weiss and Burks (Harvard U.P.)

DFT 1942 R. Levillier _Don Francisco de Toledo_ Vol. VIII (Buenos Aires: Espasa-Calpe)

VUC 1958 P. Wiener ed. _Values in a Universe of Chance_ Selected Writings of C.S. Peirce (Stanford U.P.)

TI 1961 H. Barth _Wahrheit und Ideologie_ (Zurich: Rentsch 2 ed.); Engl. tr. _Truth and Ideology_ (U. of Calif. 1976)

KHI   1968   J. Habermas <u>Knowledge</u> <u>and</u> <u>Human</u> <u>Interests</u> tr. of <u>Erkenntnis</u> <u>und</u> <u>Interesse</u> (Boston: Beacon 1971)

HLT   1969   S. Kracauer <u>History</u>. The Last Things before the Last (N.Y. Oxford)

IAI   1975   L. Feuer <u>Ideology</u> <u>and</u> <u>the</u> <u>Ideologists</u> (N.Y. Harper)

FC   1975   P. Knightly <u>The</u> <u>First</u> <u>Casualty</u> (N.Y. Harcourt Brace)

PH   1981   B. Tuchman <u>Practicing</u> <u>History</u> (N.Y. Knopf)

HT   1982   G. Graham "Can there be History of Philosophy?" <u>History</u> <u>and</u> <u>Theory</u> XXI, 1

Index

active mode of judgment 9f., 33
Adorno, T. 121
aesthetics of history 21
agency 31f.
American philosophy, N. 7, 15, 64f., 78, 88
American, N. thought 69
Analytic epistemology 1, 15-38, 130
Analytic philosophy 21ff.
Analytic style 15ff.
antecedents, and causes 113
antecedents, and consequents 31
antecedents, circumstantial or causal 23ff.
Aristotle 2f., 12, 20, 23, 31, 40, 52, 73f., 84, 98,
        102, 104, 107, 130f.
arts, as essential 69
art-and-science of history in Amer. philos. 11, 39-115,
        129-138
arts-and-sciences 2f.
assertive mode of judgment 9f., 18f., 20, 33
astrology 42
atomism, logical 132f.
Augustine 43, 58
Austen, J. 27f., 35
Ayer, A.J. 16, 37
Bacon, F. 45
Barnes, H.E. 60
Barth, H. 123, 139
Barzun, J. 11, 14
Beard, C. & M. 92, 110, 120
behavior, as active judgment 101ff.
being, historical 65-67
belief-communities 80
Bentham, J. 22
Bentley, A. 7, 103
bi-modality of history 19, 136
Bossuet, J.B 43, 58
Bradley, F.H. 59, 73, 91
Brinton, C. 61
British empiricism 4, 8
Brunschvig, L. 92
Buchanan, E. 84
Buchler, J. 3, 7, 9f., 14, 20, 37f., 57, 71f., 92, 95-
        113, 120f., 130f., 133, 139
Burckhardt, J. 128, 139
Burke, K. 27f., 37, 61
Camus, A. 5
Casas, B. de las 109, 120
Cassirer, E. 61, 103

143

particulars 133
partisans, intellectual 76ff.
past, the in Mead 53-56
Peirce, C.S. 36, 129, 134, 139
Perry, R.B. 13f.
phenomenologists 129
philosophies, imported 78
philosophy, cultural function of 70f.
philosophy, historical def. of 90
philosophy, history of 63-90
philosophy of science as theory of research 134
philosophy, modern 70ff.
philosophy not science for Schneider 63f.
Plato 3, 18, 20, 102, 110, 131
Plato, the dialogical and Socratic 130
Plato's Socrates 75
pluralism, and selectivity 41
Peirce, C.S. 22, 78
pluralism 80, 94, 131
pluralism, Santayana's 48f.
point of view, the 30f., 99
Popper, K. 94ff., 99, 120f.
positivism 16ff., 51
positivists, logical 22, 129
positivists, Vienna 16
practical knowledge 2
practical knowledge, Randall on 82f.
praxis 33
predictability 25 ff., 40
present, the in Mead 53ff.
presentational strategy 32
Pritchett, W.K. 121
proception 2f., 10, 57
proceptive parallelism 101f.
Proctor, D. 122
prophecy 33
provinciality, philosophic 88
provisionality of history 48
psychologism 4f.
query 3, 10, 20, 102, 104f.
radicals 76ff.
Randall, J.H. 15, 37, 61, 65, 70-90, 91-93, 123, 130, 132
Ranke, L. von 15, 17, 35f.
rationalists and empiricists 73f., 77
rationality 49f., 98-114
Rawlings, H.R. 122
reactionaries 76ff.
reason, as basic candor 104
reasons for, and causes of 26

About the Author

V. Tejera is Professor of Philosophy at S.U.N.Y. Stony
Brook. Other books by him are ART AND HUMAN
INTELLIGENCE (1965), ARISTOTLE'S ANALYTICS (1966),
MODES OF GREEK THOUGHT (1971), PLATO'S DIALOGUES ONE BY
ONE (1983). He is coeditor, with T. Lavine, of AGAINST
ANTIHISTORY IN PHILOSOPHY to be published by M.
Nijhoff.